THE SILENT PUNCHES

MISTI AND MILO

MOWUNMI ADE

ISBN: E-Book # 978-1-966556-44-2

Paperback # 978-1-966556-45-9

Hardcover # 978-1-966556-46-6

Printed in the United States of America

Library of Congress Reg. # 2025903891

Cover Design by: Authors Hike

Publisher: Authors Hike

For permission requests, please contact: mowunmiade.com

Table of Contents

Acknowledgment.. i

Chapter One 1

Chapter Two 14

Chapter Three 25

Chapter Four 33

Chapter Five 43

Chapter Six 53

Chapter Seven 60

Chapter Eight 67

Chapter Nine 74

Chapter Ten 84

Chapter Eleven 93

Chapter Twelve 100

Acknowledgment

My family, friends, and the outstanding team deserve immense gratitude for making this book a reality. Thank you all!

Chapter One

Awoken by the early morning clamor outside, Misti sighed, her thoughts drifting between the echoes of last night's dream and the reality of a new day beginning. It was a cloudy and cold day in March. The weather forecast had it that temperatures would be rising to the seventies later in the day. The morning, however, was still cold. Some people were seen wearing sweaters, jackets and other clothing accessories to cover themselves due to the winter-like temperatures still lurking around in the Spring. She heard the trains blasting their horns as they "uploaded and downloaded" their passengers. Almost simultaneously, the police siren was blaring from a far distance, a reminder of Busysville's constant motion.

As her eyes wandered sleepily around the ceiling of her room, suddenly, she caught a glimpse of the time from the clock on the wall of her room.

"Ah, six-ten!" she exclaimed as she jumped out of bed to join the morning rush, feeling a spark of urgency as she threw off her blankets and dashed to get ready for school.

After dressing for school, she quickly went down the stairs to check if her brother Milo was ready for school. As she got to the living room, she was greeted by their family dog, Slotty. Slotty was a golden retriever that Misti's dad, Mr. Andy Kilani, had gotten the family the previous Christmas. She wagged her tail excitedly as Misti rubbed her neck, which smelled faintly of the outdoors.

"Hello Slotty! Smart dog, look at you; you are a smarty," Misti said amusingly.

"Woof! Woof!" Slotty barked joyfully and then ran around the living room.

The living room was medium sized with walls painted light brown. The wall hangings displayed the beauty of nature and humans. There was a long old sofa big enough to seat four people, facing the brick wood fireplace seated in the middle of the wall. Its upholstery was faded but comfortable, a testament to years of family gatherings. The wall was on the opposite side of the living room. In addition to the main sofa, there was a smaller sofa placed adjacent to it. On the coffee table at the center of the room were piles of bills, magazines and other papers. The living room had been lightly furnished. The hardwood floor was squeaking as Misti walked toward the kitchen, calling out for her brother, Milo. The flooring must have seen its years due to constant walking on it.

Her house was an old four-bedroom single house in Busysville, Pennsylvania. Busysville was a small town full of the hustle and bustle of life. At the back of her house was the Busysville train station, where most of the daily noise around her house came from. From the sounds of people chattering at the train station to the loud noise from the train horns, the Kilanis were accustomed to living with the noise. They had lived in the neighborhood for nineteen years! It was a small town with a big personality, bustling with people who moved with purpose.

"Good morning, Milo!" Misti greeted him.

"I hope you had a nice sleep," she added.

"Um, not really," Milo replied, poking half-heartedly at his breakfast.

"Is there a problem?" asked Misti.

"Kind of …," he replied.

Milo muttered to himself. Misti looked at Milo with worry as he muttered to himself. He paused, glanced at Misti and finally voiced his concerns.

"Misti, I feel like not going to school today or anymore," he said sadly. Misti looked shocked and confused about what Milo had just told her.

"I feel anxious and sad," he expressed. "I feel pressured by dad and mom to get great grades. If I don't, I feel like I am failing them and myself," he added.

"No, you are not!" Misti interjected. Her voice was gentle but firm. She could see now how much he had been bottling up.

"I am scared of letting Dad and Mom know about it; that is why I have kept things to myself for some time, and I didn't think that anyone would get it or get me," he explained.

"I am not doing too well in my Math and Science classes as they expect, although I am not failing. I have another test in both classes today, and I think I might not get above ninety percent in both as they always want. So, it's better that I stay home today pretending to be sick," he added.

"So how will doing that going to solve the problem? Aren't you not going to take those tests still?" Misti asked, wondering. She continued preparing their sandwiches, letting his words sink in. She took a deep breath, choosing her words carefully.

"If that works for you today, I bet it's not going to work forever. I don't think that is the right way to go or the right thing to do," she stated emphatically.

As she handed him his sandwich, she gave him a small, reassuring smile. "I think it's better to go in, do your best, and wait to see the results. You're not alone in this—you've got me, Mom, and Dad. And none of us would want you to feel this way."

Milo sighed as he sat on the kitchen stool. He pondered whether to take the advice of his sister or not. His mind wandered, torn between his sister's encouraging words and his own lingering doubts. He looked very worried and sad. Slotty came to him, curled her legs around his legs, and began to whimper. She threw her head against Milo's legs. She ran to her toys, came back with one of them and dropped it in between Milo's legs. She showed him that she felt his pain and was trying to comfort him at the same time. Her tail wagged slowly as if trying to comfort him, and a flicker of gratitude crossed Milo's face as he softened. This lightened Milo's mood, and he began to rub Slotty's back softly.

"Thanks, Slotty, for caring," he said as he continued to rub the dog's back and neck. The dog sat calmly and quietly in front of him.

"It's seven-fifteen," Misti announced. "We better get going. Otherwise, we would be late for school," she added as she handed Milo the sandwich she had made him.

"Milo, don't worry, you will be fine," she assured him. "You will ace your test, I believe," she assured him.

"Um … I hope so," he shrugged.

"You studied, right?" she asked.

"Er … yes … I will go then," he replied hesitantly, a mix of worry and resolution crossing his face as he stood up.

As Milo and Misti were walking down the street, they found a homeless man sitting beside the tent he had made as his temporary home. He was begging for alms as people were walking in haste to catch up to whatever pursuit the day had to offer them. The man thought he could get at least some people to stop and give him some attention by either giving him some money or at least replying to his greetings.

"Good morning, God bless you," the homeless man said anytime someone passed by him. Some people did not look at him at all, and others dropped some coins to be in the act of giving. Milo and Misti passed by this man every day they went to school.

"Good morning, God bless you," the man said to Milo and Misti as usual.

"Good morning, Mr. Freedman," Milo and Misti replied as they passed by him.

Mr. Freedman was a veteran who had a normal life before his life took a downward spiral. A few years prior, he was deployed to Iraq to work as an engineer on warplanes. Before his deployment, he had been the support for his wife because she had been suffering from multiple sclerosis. His three children were just two, three and five. But his life took a heartbreaking turn a few years ago. Word around Busysville had it that Mr. Freedman had struggled with his mental health after receiving news of his wife's sudden death. Unable to process the loss, his world began to unravel.

Rumor held that he was unable to return to his post in Iraq, having failed the mental health screening. The government offered him an administrative assignment at the military base in Glendale, Pennsylvania. That job, as the tale had it, did not last because it was claimed that he was underperforming. Eventually, he was released from the military. That was when things started getting out of hand. Within months he lost his job, and he lost his house as well because he could not afford to pay for his mortgage. He then lost his three children to a foster home. When it was discovered that he was not mentally fit to take care of his three children, Child Protective Services took his children from him and sent them to a foster home. His other family members did not live close enough to help him with the children. Most of them were living in Europe.

The fact that his children were taken from him was the last straw to his predicament. He ended up on the streets of Busysville. He had been evacuated many times before he found the piece of space where he pitched his tent. The space was an extension of the Busysville train station. The piece of land was adjacent to Simpson Street. He had been living at the other end of Simpson Street for about six months. His tent was a block from Milo and Misti's house. Sometimes, Mrs. Klara Kilani would prepare some warm food and give it to him. Some other neighbors used to help him in one way or another as well. Last winter, people brought him jackets, gloves, socks and a comforter set to keep him warm during the freezing temperatures. The community looked out for Mr. Freedman as best they could, but even their care was only a patch on the hardship he endured.

Just then, a cheerful voice called out, breaking the quiet of the early morning bustle.

"Mr. Freedman!" a little boy shouted and waved as his mom walked him to school.

"Hey, W-a-u-n-a-k-e-e!" Mr. Freedman replied, singing out the boy's name.

"My mom bought me a cool toy. It is a train, just like that one over there," Waunakee pointed to the train that had just arrived at the Busysville train station.

"Choo Choo," he demonstrated, mimicking the train's whistle as he continued animatedly telling Mr. Freedman all about his new toy train, his small face lighting up with excitement.

A soft smile crossed Mr. Freedman's face as he listened to the boy, his weathered features briefly lightening with the innocence of the moment. For a few seconds, he seemed to forget his troubles, caught up in Waunakee's joy.

"Hey buddy, let's not bother Mr. Freedman," his mom finally told him.

"Oh … okay," he said.

"Oh … no … no, he is no bother at all. He brightens my day," Mr. Freedman smiled.

"He makes me remember my three children – Glay, Flint and Ava. I know that one day, I will see them again," His voice softened as if the words carried a quiet, fragile hope.

"Have a nice day, ma'am … and buddy," he told them as he smiled.

"I will bring my toy train tomorrow to share with you," Waunakee told him excitedly.

"All right … thank you," Mr. Freedman answered. There was a flicker of genuine gratitude in his gaze as he watched them walk away.

"Bye!" Waunakee called out, glancing over his shoulder as he followed his mother down the bustling sidewalk.

Mrs. Aiyana Poole, Waunakee's mother, had navigated life as a single mother with quiet determination since her son was an infant. She'd been just twenty-two when her husband left her, disappearing from her life with little warning, leaving her with Waunakee, who was now five. She could recall that day with painful clarity—how ordinary everything had seemed until it wasn't.

The day began like any regular day for the Pooles. Mr. Chayton Poole, twenty-five, was dressed up for work. He had the French roast coffee with creamer and croissant as he watched the morning news as usual.

"What's today's weather forecast?" Aiyana asked him.

"It's going to be raining and storming today with warm temperatures in the sixties," Chayton replied.

"Oh… alright," Aiyana responded. "I'll need to run some errands before it starts. Do you remember when they said the rain would begin?"

"The reporter said around eleven this morning," he replied.

"That's good. I will have had enough time to run some errands and come back before it would start," she said.

"Remember to take your lunch along … I packed it, and it is on the countertop," she told him, pointing to the countertop in the kitchen.

"Thanks, I will not forget to take it," Chayton replied as he stood up to leave for work. He went to the crib at the corner of the room where the baby was lying, and he kissed him as usual. He was fast asleep. Waunakee used to be up in the middle of the night eating and crying for one thing or another. However, early in the morning, when the sun was rising, he would sleep soundly, away from all the crying in the middle of the night.

Their tiny living room was simple but cozy, with only a sofa facing the TV, a worn side chair in the corner, and bright curtains that made the room seem larger. In the small nursery, which served as Waunakee's room, the walls were painted a cheerful white, adorned with animal decals. Aiyana had picked out light blue jacquard curtains with tiny floral prints for the window, adding a touch of charm to the space. A changing table and rocking chair sat by the crib, where the baby's clothes and supplies were neatly organized on a small shelf within reach. The space was modest but full of love, each item carefully chosen and arranged by Aiyana.

"I am running late. I need to go now to escape the heavy traffic," Chayton told his wife.

"Okay, honey, take care of yourself," his wife said.

"Bye, and take care of yourself as well," he said.

"Drive safe," she added.

"I will," he said as he put his lunch in his work bag and kissed his wife. He then walked out of the door.

That was the last time his wife had set her eyes on him. In the evening, when it was his usual time to come home, he never did. Aiyana was worried why he was not home yet because it was unlike him. She thought it might have been due to the heavy traffic because of the rush hour - people were trying to get back home. However, when his arrival was way past his usual time without any phone calls, then she started to panic. She felt that something bad might have happened to her husband. She thought he might have been involved in an accident, and nobody knew who to call yet. Bad thoughts of all the worst possible reasons he had not been home started to flood her thought process. She looked at her phone multiple times just to see if there were text messages or phone calls, but nothing. She then decided to call her mom to inform her of what was going on.

"Hello mom, Chayton has not come home from work … it is very unlike him to stay out late," she sounded worried.

"Hello, darling. I hope you guys did not have an argument before he left for work in the morning?" the mom asked her.

"No… we didn't fight at all," Aiyana replied, a slight catch in her voice. She could barely hold back the flood of worry that had consumed her.

"Let's give him some more time … he might have been stuck at work or something. Don't worry, he will be home soon," her mom encouraged her.

"That he did not call at all is why I am worried about it," she pointed out.

"Maybe his phone battery died," her mom suggested, though Aiyana could sense a hint of worry in her mother's tone as well. "Let's just hope he's back soon."

"If by tomorrow morning I do not hear from him, I will be calling his work. It's late to call his work now, it's ten-thirty. They are closed," Aiyana told her mom.

"Alright, sweetheart. We'll do just that tomorrow morning. I'll come over and be with you for it," her mom offered, her words soothing the unease that had settled deep within Aiyana. "Try to get some sleep, baby, and take care of little Wauna for me," she added, using the family's affectionate nickname for Waunakee.

"All right … good night, Mom," Aiyana said.

"Good night, sweetheart," Mrs. Alberty said.

It was a long night for Aiyana. She waited for her husband because she could not sleep. She had a gut feeling that something bad was happening to her. She sat on the rocking chair, rocking herself to sleep. She eventually dozed off while waiting for her husband. The cry of Waunakee woke her up from her sleep. She looked at the time, and it was one in the morning. She felt heavy and sad because her husband was still not back. She attended to her baby and planned out how that day would go.

In the morning, her mom, Mrs. Alberty, arrived. It was seven-ten. She helped Aiyana with the baby while she called her husband's job one hour later.

After a few rings, Chayton's boss picked up, his voice calm and businesslike. But when Aiyana explained why she was calling, his tone shifted. "No, Mrs. Poole, he's not here yet," he replied. "Actually, we've been waiting for him to arrive as well—he was supposed to oversee a project today. We haven't heard from him."

Aiyana nodded numbly, her stomach sinking further. She relayed this to her mother, her voice subdued.

"Mom, if by afternoon I don't hear from him, I will need to report it to the police," Aiyana announced.

"I understand … but they would ask you if he had been gone for twenty-four hours since he is an adult. If it had not been twenty-four hours yet, they would not have done anything about it. Let's wait twenty-four hours before we go to the police. Meanwhile, we can call all his friends and family members to ask if they heard anything from him or about him," her mom advised.

"All right, Mom… I will search through the phone numbers I have on my phone to make those calls," Aiyana Poole said.

In the end, Aiyana did not know the whereabouts of her husband and none of the people she called knew either. When twenty-four hours had passed, she went to the police station to report the incident. The police and the community did their best to look for Mr. Chayton Poole, but all to no avail. He never showed up to work, either. The police never got any reports of accidents or unusual occurrences that might have involved him.

Aiyana clung to hope as best she could despite the reality growing colder and harder each day. She held on for Waunakee's sake, choosing to believe that Chayton was alive, somewhere, even if it felt like her heart was shrinking each day he remained missing. But as months passed, that hope began to fade, like a candle flickering in the wind.

Then, one afternoon, about six months after her husband had been missing, the mail guy brought their mail, and she found an unusual letter among them. The letter was addressed to her. She was eager to know what was inside the envelope. She opened it, and to her surprise, it was from Chayton Poole. It read as follows:

My dear Aiyana,

I am so sorry for all the pain that I have caused you through these past few months. I want you to know that I am alive. I don't think that I am mentally ready to be a father. I know that it is very selfish of me to leave you and our son. Please find it in your heart to forgive me. Take care of Waunakee. Maybe someday I will be back. I still love you …

Chayton

Aiyana cried out her eyes after she read the letter. Her heart was pounding so fast that she thought it was going to stop. Her skin turned pale immediately, and her hands were shaking. She became sick for a few weeks thereafter. She had to work with a therapist before she decided to accept the reality of her plight. Chayton never sent any other letter after the one he sent, and he never came back.

Chapter Two

Misti was eighteen years old. She was in twelfth grade at Swiftly High School. Milo attended the middle school at the same school as Misti. He was fourteen years old. He was in eighth grade. Swiftly Middle and High School was a public school for students in sixth to twelfth grade. It was a popular school that most children in the area attended, and it was under the Hilltown school district—a popular and sought-after school district by parents. That was because the school had ranked first in terms of quality education in their county—Effexshire County. Mr. and Mrs. Kilani were paying a fortune in mortgage to live within that school district, believing that good education was a key to life and future opportunities.

It was a bright morning. The clouds looked beautiful as the sun shone through them. The day brought a refreshing atmosphere that gave way to the early morning cool breeze. The birds were chirping in excitement at the beauty around them, filling the air with their joyful sounds. As usual in Busysville, the noise was already up. The trains, the cars, people chatting, animals sounding for whatever reason, and the school buses were already heard passing by; some students were walking to school, eager to start their day.

It was seven thirty-eight. At Swiftly Middle School, the students were standing around their lockers, chatting and getting ready for the school day.

"Hey Milo!" shouted Ravesh.

"Hey," Milo replied.

"Ah … I hope you are ready for today's tests!" Ravesh exclaimed.

"Um … I am not too sure about that," Milo replied. "We'll see," he added, feeling a mix of anxiety and anticipation.

"Why not? I know that you will do well, man," Ravesh encouraged him with a reassuring smile.

"For me … I cannot wait to prove myself to my dad, especially my stepmom," he continued, expressing his desire for validation from his family.

"What do you want to prove to her?" Milo asked.

"That I will become successful in life … it's just a matter of time," Ravesh said, smiling, reflecting the aspirations many young people have as they navigate their educational journeys and personal growth.

"She told my dad to give up on me. She taunts me every day that I will never amount to anything," he said, his voice filled with frustration and hurt.

"Wow … that's negative … I thought my issues were the biggest in the world," Milo shared, surprised by Ravesh's situation.

"I am doing well on my tests, but they want perfect scores. That is what is stressing me out," he continued, revealing the pressure he felt to meet his parents' high expectations.

"The difference between you and me is that you have your mom around," Ravesh expressed, a hint of longing in his voice. "I wished my mom had stayed. I don't blame her, though … because she could not stand my dad's meanness anymore. He treated her badly. He then went on to remarry … to a Jezebel. That woman is pure evil, Milo. Her children are little meanies," he lamented, clearly feeling the weight of his family dynamics.

"I have another issue with my parents," Milo announced, shifting the focus back to himself.

"You know I play football, right?" he asked. "I don't like playing football. My dad is the one forcing me to do the sport. I like to play piano, but he believes playing piano as a guy is too soft. He feels that guys must do tough stuff, such as playing soccer, football, or basketball," he continued, frustration evident in his tone.

"He often compares me with his friends' children—how they were involved in sports while in middle and high school and how they got a full scholarship ride to attend college," Milo added, feeling the pressure of those comparisons weighing heavily on him.

"That's a tough one, buddy," Ravesh replied sympathetically, understanding the struggle of parental expectations.

"Sometimes, I wonder why parents don't get it," Ravesh pointed out thoughtfully, reflecting on the generational gap in understanding.

"They like to compare how they spent their lives growing up with ours," Ravesh continued, shaking his head in disbelief at the disconnect between their experiences and those of their parents.

"Exactly! My parents are the same way, too. Especially my mom; I don't know how many times she has recounted some stories of her struggles growing up," Milo said, laughing lightly despite the frustration underlying his words. "It's like they forget that times have changed, and so have we."

"She would start by saying, 'Wow … children of this generation, you are spoiled. Life is too easy for you! When we were growing up, we did not have everything you guys enjoy today. No internet, no social media, and few old games; some of my friends did not even have television in their homes."

"You were forced to walk to school—no matter the distance or weather conditions," Milo said, mimicking his mom with a dramatic flair.

"You guys have everything, everything. So, what do you want to complain about?" My mom would ask. "For children of your age who grew up on the farm, you would be forced to wake up by four in the morning," she'd continued, emphasizing the stark differences in their experiences.

"What time do you always wake up, Milo? Around six o'clock every morning, right? You see, you have it easy today compared to back then … you have no excuse to say you are feeling any pressure. Tell me, what pressures? … on the good life you have," she would say mockingly," Milo recounted, rolling his eyes at the memory.

"The scariest part is when she tells me that back then, children my age were already working to feed their parents and siblings," Milo pointed out, his tone shifting to one of disbelief. "That always makes me wonder: how could parents expect a fourteen-year-old to be feeding them? Are they not the parents? Isn't it their job to take care of the children? Thank God that was back then. I don't think that would work now," Milo said jokingly, trying to lighten the heavy topic.

"That is one good thing about our generation. Life is no longer as it used to be. There is more freedom for us," Ravesh said with a laugh. "I would not have survived their generation. I think it was a mean one for them, so they think

17

we should experience the same … but not me," he added with a grin, clearly relieved by the differences in their upbringing.

"I hear you, buddy … their own parents forced things on them, so they believe they can do the same to us," Milo replied thoughtfully. "That is one thing those parents are not getting: times have changed, and so have we. We face our own challenges that are just as valid."

"You have no idea how I feel with all their preachings and pushing. They think they are trying to help. I understand that they are trying to do their job as parents. They want their children to make it big in life—to be rich, famous, and make something good out of life. However, they are hurting rather than helping if the pressures and comparisons are too much," Milo stated, his frustration evident.

"Ravesh … sometimes, I can't sleep; I have headaches, and I panic. They are pushing me too hard—especially when exams and tests are around the corner, just like today. I try my best to study as hard as I can, just to avoid my parents' tales of how children back then could handle any situation while the ones of nowadays cannot," Milo expressed, revealing the toll that pressure was taking on his mental health.

"Don't worry, my friend; relax. Don't let those pressures of making things perfect weigh you down," Ravesh advised, trying to offer some comfort. "In my case, it's like I am living among wolves … I do my thing and … I try not to think too much about it," he continued, sharing his own coping mechanism for dealing with the stress.

Milo and Ravesh both laughed as they discussed their plights, finding humor in their shared experiences. It was eight o'clock.

"Drrrrrr"—the school bell rang, cutting through their conversation.

"I feel better now that we talked about it. I am going to do my best in today's tests. Even if I don't get a perfect score like my parents would want, I will not think too much about it, as you have told me to do," Milo told his friend with renewed determination.

"Thanks, man," Milo expressed gratefully.

"Don't mention it; what are friends for?" Ravesh asked with humor, lightening the mood even further.

"We will talk at lunch, and good luck on the tests!" Ravesh added cheerfully.

"I wish you the same," Milo replied sincerely.

"Hey, watch where you are going!" Milo told one of the students who almost bumped into him in the hallway as he and Ravesh hurriedly made their way to their separate homerooms, navigating the bustling crowd of students eager to start their day.

At lunchtime, the students were seen in long lines waiting to get their food. Some who did not have the patience to wait for the warm meals grabbed items from the grab-and-go section. Some students were sitting in groups chatting, while others were by themselves, lost in their thoughts. The students had twenty-five minutes for lunch every day, a time allotment that did not please them. They believed that the time was insufficient for them to stand in line and then rush to eat their food.

"Hi, Eddy … have you seen Milo?" Pravesh asked, scanning the cafeteria.

"Em … no, oh, there he is," Eddy said as he looked up and pointed to Milo, who was making his way through the crowd.

"Hey, buddy. You know my class is a long walk from here," Milo said as he joined his friends at their table.

"I don't know why the school cannot give us at least forty-five minutes to relax and enjoy our food," he complained, frustration evident in his voice.

"Now, I must wait in line for another ten minutes. What time do I have left to eat? … You guys are lucky that your classroom is closer to the cafeteria," he said as he turned to Ravesh and Eddy, who nodded in agreement.

"I will be right back," he told his friends as he went to grab one of the grab-and-go meals, hoping it would be enough to tide him over.

"Back already?" Eddy asked him as he approached them with a plastic container in hand.

"I told you I didn't have the time to stay in line; before you know it, lunchtime will be over. I just got the grab-and-go meal. It doesn't taste great, but it's better than nothing. Ugh … my head hurts … I didn't eat anything before leaving home this morning because I was too scared about today's tests. Now I … feel very hungry," he told them, rubbing his temples in frustration.

"Hmmm, that reminds me—how were your tests?" Ravesh asked him, genuinely curious about how Milo had fared under the pressure.

"I took the Math test. It was not bad. I will be taking the Art test after we leave here. I don't like Art, and I just want to get that off my mind right now. Otherwise, I might not be able to enjoy my lunch. I told you this morning about my parents' expectations regarding my academic performance. I better do well on the Art test," he told Ravesh, unwrapping his lunch with a sigh of resignation.

"Yes ... you're right," Ravesh replied, understanding the pressure Milo felt.

"Most of my concerns are about their validation of anything I do … which is exhausting," Milo added with a smirk, trying to lighten the mood despite his frustrations.

"My battles are with my siblings … dang … they can be very annoying, especially my older brother," Eddy jumped in, eager to share his own struggles.

"He is a snitch, a big tattle-tale. I don't like that guy … it's not nice to have him as a brother. Last night, he snitched on me that I was on my iPad past the time we were asked to put our devices away. That was not true, but it landed me in trouble with my mom," he explained, shaking his head in disbelief. "Another incident happened last week … we wear the same size shoes … he knew my Fastbreeze sneakers were my favorite. When I was going home from school, I saw him chatting with his friends. Guess what he was wearing? … my Fastbreeze shoes! And there are so many other annoying things he does that make my parents take his side," he lamented, his friends laughing as he recounted his ordeal.

"You guys don't know how much this hurts," he told his friends as they laughed even more, finding humor in his misfortune.

"That's sibling rivalry … bruh … it's common," Ravesh told him knowingly, nodding in sympathy.

"I don't have a brother … so I cannot know how you feel, Eddy," Milo told him jokingly, trying to lighten the atmosphere further while appreciating the bond they shared over their respective family challenges.

"In my case, it's my stepmom and her two kids. She tries everything to make my dad dislike me. She lies about little things just to get me in trouble with him. The other time, she lied that I broke one of her son's toys. Do I look like someone who would be playing with a five-year-old kid's toy? ... I am fourteen and going to high school in a few months," he said, his frustration palpable.

"I did not get an allowance for the following week because of that lie. Also, my house chores were increased," he added, eliciting laughter from his friends as they commiserated with him.

"Most times, in my absence, her children would come into my room, scatter my bed, and move my books. They would go into my closet, pull down my neatly hung clothes, and throw my shoes off the rack. I dare not complain. The time I did, she told me that I lacked empathy and that I had issues connecting with other people," he explained, shaking his head in disbelief.

"Oh no ... no ... that's bad! Even I wouldn't take that. How could she allow that or think it was okay for her kids to do?" Milo asked him, genuinely shocked by the situation.

"I don't know. I do not blame her; I blame my dad for giving her all the power in the world to do whatever she likes in that house. The worst part is that anytime my grandma or anyone from the family visits, she acts nicely toward me, putting on a show as if she is looking out for me or, let's say, taking care of me ... my dad does that as well. This angers me the most," Ravesh said, his voice filled with frustration and hurt.

"I have called my mom several times to come and take me away, but her new husband does not want me to live with them," Ravesh continued, his expression a mix of longing and despair as he considered the complexities of his family situation.

"What? That is too bad … and your mom did nothing about it?" Milo asked, surprised by Ravesh's situation.

"Yep, she even makes excuses for him any time I bring it up for her to come get me. She gave me the excuse that her husband told her he was not ready to raise another man's child, especially if my dad was still alive, and that it was not his responsibility, but my dad's," he explained to his friends, his tone filled with disappointment.

"That is kind of true, though …," Eddy said, considering the complexities of family dynamics.

"A mom should be able to fight for her son. I don't think my mom would do that to me," Milo said firmly, expressing his belief in maternal support.

"The fact that my mom made it known that her new husband does not want me to live with them gives my stepmom the opportunity to ridicule me anytime she wants. She says that no one wants me, and that why would she want me or be nice to me if my own mother does not want me?" he continued, his voice heavy with emotion as he shared the pain of feeling unwanted.

"You see why you should still be thankful, Milo; some folks are facing bigger challenges. I am not saying that your issues with your parents are not important as well," Eddy said, trying to offer perspective.

"You are right; I should be …" Milo agreed, reflecting on his own situation in light of Ravesh's struggles.

Just then, the bell rang, signaling that lunchtime was over. All the students were seen getting up and heading back to their classes, a mix of chatter and laughter filling the hallway as they returned to their routines.

Chapter Three

When Misti walked into homeroom, a group of students were giggling. She wondered what they were laughing about but didn't dwell on it. Soon enough, she noticed why—someone had written "loser" on her chair.

Misti was a star student, well-known at Swiftly High School. Part of her reputation came from her father's popularity in Busysville and the surrounding towns. Secondly, her mother was an attorney specializing in employment law and known for representing employees wronged by their employers over wages, discrimination, harassment, or retaliation.

But Misti was respected in her own right. She was a straight-A student and actively involved in extracurriculars, including tennis, serving as Girls' Club secretary, and as president of the Student Affairs Committee. She also participated in volunteer programs and internships. To some students, she was a role model; to others, a source of envy.

"Who wrote 'loser' on my chair?" Misti asked, looking around expectantly. The class fell silent.

"Misti, is everything okay?" Ms. Williams asked, noticing her reaction.

"No, Ms. Williams. Someone wrote 'loser' on my chair, and I don't know who it was," Misti replied sadly, her voice cracking.

Ms. Keisha Williams, their homeroom teacher, had only recently joined Swiftly High School. At twenty-five, she'd been teaching Biology and Chemistry to the tenth and eleventh graders for about three months. When she first introduced herself to the class, she encouraged her students to believe in themselves and not let any obstacle hold them back, reminding them that they were preparing for higher education or other future pursuits. She had even shared some of the challenges she'd faced to get where she was.

Ms. Williams had told the class that she was the first in her family to attend college. Her father had worked for the post office in Alabama for decades before retiring, and her mom was a hairdresser. With four siblings—two brothers and two sisters—she was the middle child. She explained that watching her older brother and sister struggle financially after high school motivated her to take a different path by furthering her education to improve her own life and help her family.

At an early age, Ms. Williams had learned to do hair by watching her mom work on clients in a small shop near their home in Alabama. Soon, she began doing her friends' hair as a side business, earning a little money that she saved toward her college education. Her parents had already told her that they couldn't afford to send her to college, even with government aid and scholarships, so she knew she'd have to find a way to fund it herself.

Ms. Williams was accepted into Wise Community College, which was close enough for her to commute from home. To support herself, she took on an additional job alongside her hair business. She found work at a nonprofit organization nearby, which provided assistance for people struggling with substance abuse, supported domestic violence victims, helped people with disabilities find employment, and offered general humanitarian services like food and personal supplies for those in need. Though the pay was low, the job was fulfilling; she found it refreshing to be able to make a difference in people's lives while earning a small income. She stayed with the organization for years.

She later attended Rock University, also in Alabama, to complete her studies in Biology and Chemistry. After graduating, she found a job as a laboratory technician in a small local lab. While working there, Ms. Williams continued her education, returning to earn a master's degree in Biology and Chemistry. She had always wanted to be a teacher, so after completing her master's, she decided to move to Pennsylvania. There, she obtained her teaching license and was hired at Swiftly High School, marking the start of her teaching career.

"Attention, everyone! Who wrote 'loser' on Misti's chair?" Ms. Williams demanded, looking around the room.

No one responded. Some students looked down, trying to hide smirks and giggles; others avoided her gaze, pretending not to understand, while a few genuinely seemed unaware of the situation.

"If no one tells me who did this, I'll assume you're all responsible. I'll march the entire class to the principal's office, where each of you will receive thirty demerit points. I'll also be sending a notification to your parents," she announced sternly. As she spoke, Diego, one of the students, raised his hand.

"Ms. Williams, I know who did it. I don't want to get into trouble with my parents because I've already had enough demerits this semester. I don't want to take the fall for what somebody else did," Diego pointed out.

As Diego spoke, whispers spread around the classroom. Some students murmured that Diego was a tattle-tale.

"What did you get demerits for?" one student asked him. Turning around, Diego saw that it was Latoya who had asked.

"I got in trouble for smoking in the bathroom … and, well, there were also some narcotics and a few strong drinks found in my bag," he replied with a touch of sarcasm.

"Oooh," the other students exclaimed, some laughing.

"Silence!" Ms. Williams ordered. "I will not tolerate any unruly behavior in this class," she added firmly.

"You're all acting like children. You are seniors for crying out loud! Soon, you'll be graduating to pursue your dreams. Is this how you want to behave in the real world?" she asked, her tone stern.

After reprimanding the class, she turned her attention back to Diego.

"Diego, who wrote 'loser' on Misti's chair?" she asked him directly.

"Lucas did, Ms. Williams," Diego replied.

"Uh … sorry for ratting you out, buddy, but I really don't want to get into any more trouble with the school or my parents," he apologized to Lucas.

"You don't need to apologize if he actually did it," Ms. Williams cut in sharply.

"Lucas, is that true?" she asked, turning her attention to him.

Lucas sighed, glancing at Ms. Williams with wide, alert eyes and a forced smile. He hesitated, clearly reluctant to answer, but quickly realized Ms. Williams wasn't backing down.

"Um, I ... I ... did it, Ms. Williams," he finally admitted, his voice barely audible.

"Well ... I'm so...rry," he added slowly.

"You'll be sorry soon enough," she replied. "You're going to the principal's office to explain your actions."

Then Ms. Williams turned to Misti. "Misti, is this the first time Lucas has harassed you, or has this been happening for a while?" she asked.

"Um ... sometimes he makes cutting remarks about me, but I usually just ignore him. This is the first time he's actually violated my space by writing on my chair," Misti said, her voice tight with anger as she looked at Lucas.

"Okay, we're done here," Ms. Williams said firmly. "Lucas, pack your things and let's go."

"Misti, you'll need to come to the principal's office as well to make a statement about what's been happening between you two. You don't need to pack your things," she explained.

"Class, I'll be back shortly. You'd better behave," she warned, giving them a stern look.

With that, Ms. Williams, Lucas, and Misti headed to the principal's office. Inside, Mr. Hue Cheng, the principal, was sorting through a stack of papers on his desk. Mr. Cheng was a seasoned educator with decades of experience in teaching and administration. According to reports, he came from a wealthy family of real estate magnates in China and was their only child. His parents had sent him to the United States to study medicine when he was just eighteen, but once here, he discovered a passion for teaching.

Eventually, he switched from medicine to Biology, which displeased his parents. They had hoped he would pursue a prestigious career as a doctor. Despite their repeated attempts to persuade him to return to medicine, he made it clear that he'd rather teach science. When they saw he wouldn't change his mind, they cut off his financial support. From that point on, Mr. Cheng supported himself to complete his degree in Biology—a decision that would set him on the path to his career in education.

Mr. Cheng's office was located near the library, just down the hallway from Ms. Williams's classroom and adjacent to the science laboratory. The office was spacious, with a large desk at the center surrounded by chairs for visitors. To the left were bookshelves neatly filled with books, while storage closets for office supplies and materials lined the right wall. In one corner of the room, two planters with lush English Ivy added a touch of greenery and helped purify the air.

"Good morning, Principal Cheng," they all greeted as they entered.

"Good morning, everyone," Mr. Cheng replied warmly. "Ms. Williams, what brings you all here today?"

Ms. Williams recounted the incident in class and then invited Lucas and Misti to explain any prior issues they might have had with each other.

"Who would like to go first?" Principal Cheng asked, looking between the two students.

"I will," Misti volunteered.

"Principal Cheng, Lucas has been jealous of me ever since I won the 'Student of the Month' award four times in a row. I don't understand why that should cause any friction.

I believe every student has an equal chance to win the award if they work hard, which I did," she explained calmly.

"We used to study together," Misti continued. "But I started noticing a change in his attitude toward me. He began making untrue comments and cutting remarks about me. Eventually, I couldn't take it anymore, so I decided to distance myself. I didn't want the added stress, especially since I already have my own personal issues to deal with."

"What kind of remarks did he make?" Mr. Cheng asked.

"Um … things like, 'you cheated,' or 'you don't deserve the award,' and so on," she replied.

"I decided it was best to just block it out and walk away whenever he started in on me to avoid his negativity. That's all," Misti concluded.

Mr. Cheng then turned to Lucas for his side of the story.

"Lucas, what do you have to say in response to what Misti just shared?" Mr. Cheng asked.

"I admit I got jealous of her winning the 'Student of the Month' award four times in a row," Lucas said, his tone contrite. "Her winning has created a big problem for me at home because my parents haven't been too happy with me," he explained.

"They compare me to Misti, taunting me that she's smarter than I am," Lucas continued. "The worst part is that our parents are friends, so they often see each other and talk about Misti and me."

"That's all I have to say," he added, his voice tinged with sadness.

"Alright," Mr. Cheng said. "I'll need to call your parents. Your behavior is unacceptable. You're suspended for two days. Hopefully, this will give you time to reflect on your actions and learn how to behave more appropriately in the future."

"Misti, I'll be calling your parents as well to let them know what happened. In the meantime, you can go back to class," he informed her.

"Okay, thank you, Mr. Cheng," she replied, nodding.

"Lucas, you'll wait here while I call your parents to come pick you up," Mr. Cheng announced.

"Thank you, Ms. Williams, for bringing this to my attention," he added, appreciating her involvement.

"My pleasure!" she replied with a smile.

Ms. Williams and Misti returned to the classroom while Lucas stayed behind in the principal's office, waiting for his parents to arrive.

Chapter Four

It was an early Saturday evening in April. The bright daylight was slowly giving way to the gentle embrace of nightfall. A soft breeze blew, cooling the lingering warmth left by the sun's rays. Trees swayed rhythmically as if dancing to the whispers of the light wind. Birds flitted between branches—some chirping melodiously, adding to the evening's symphony, while others seemed to chatter amongst themselves. Nearby, squirrels darted playfully, chasing one another and savoring the final moments of the day's warmth.

In the Busysville neighborhood, most residents knew each other. Although it was a small town, its energy lived up to its name. Its strategic location near the bustling Busysville Train Station and major roadways made it a hub of activity. The town boasted a variety of businesses: restaurants, bakeries, convenience stores, pharmacies, a hair salon, a barber shop, grocery stores, gas stations, clothing stores, print shops, mechanic garages—nearly everything you could need, scattered across its vibrant streets.

At the heart of the town stood the town hall, affectionately named "Center Stage." Right next door was the post office, the only one in Busysville, always teeming with activity. The constant hum of life defined the town's character.

But Busysville wasn't just about commerce and activity. The town had a rich spiritual side, with various religious organizations representing denominations like Baptist, Evangelical, and more. Most businesses shut their doors on Sundays, granting the town a rare respite from its usual hustle. Sundays in Busysville were for peace, worship, and rest—a welcome pause for the hardworking "Busysvillians."

"Busysville should expect some light showers in the early hours of tomorrow," the local news reporter announced on the television, her voice cutting through the evening calm.

Mr. Kilani had been relaxing, watching the evening news. He was a dedicated medical doctor at St. Mary's Hospital, the only hospital in Herostown—a city just outside of Busysville. His job often kept him busy, but evenings like this allowed him to unwind. Mrs. Klara Kilani, on the other hand, was an accomplished attorney and a partner at the well-renowned law firm in Busysville, *Levi, Ekene, and Klara Associates*. The couple had met years ago as students at the University of Moonstone in Pennsylvania, a time they often reminisced about with fondness.

"Misti!" Mr. Kilani called out, glancing toward the kitchen, where the faint clatter of pots and pans could be heard.

"Coming, Dad," Misti replied cheerfully, her high-pitched voice carrying over the noise.

Misti had been helping her mom prepare dinner, a regular family tradition on weekends. She quickly wiped her hands on a kitchen towel and walked into the living room to see what her dad needed.

"Are you doing okay … with what happened between you and Lucas yesterday?" Mr. Kilani asked gently, concern stamped on his face.

"Yes, I am," Misti replied with a reassuring smile. "It's the least of my worries, Dad. I understand he acted that way out of jealousy. I would've been jealous too, but I wouldn't go to the length of writing 'loser' on his chair—that was uncalled for."

Her dad nodded, appreciating her maturity. Before he could respond, Mrs. Kilani's voice rang out from the kitchen.

"Andy, can we talk about that later?" she called out. "I need Misti's help here with the lasagna."

"Okay, go help your mother," Mr. Kilani said with a warm smile. "We'll talk about this later. I'm just glad you're okay."

"All right, Dad," Misti replied before heading back to the kitchen.

Misti rejoined her mom, who was busy arranging ingredients on the countertop. The smell of fresh herbs and tangy tomato sauce filled the air.

"Honey, turn on the oven and set it to 400 degrees Fahrenheit," Mrs. Kilani instructed, her voice calm but firm.

"Once preheated, please put the lasagna in for thirty minutes without the lid. It should already be softened, right?" she asked, pausing to glance at her daughter.

"Yes, Mom, it's soft," Misti confirmed, carefully checking the dish.

"Good. Later, you'll cover the pan with the lid to bake for another twenty minutes. I want it to be perfectly cooked, not burnt. So, keep an eye on it," Klara added, her tone both instructive and affectionate.

Misti smiled, feeling a sense of pride in helping her mom with a family favorite. Moments like these were what made weekends special.

"By the time the lasagna is ready, I'll be done frying the chicken," Misti's mom said as she moved closer to the stove to check on the sizzling chicken.

"Okay, Mom," Misti replied, watching her work.

"We're making more food than usual. Are we expecting visitors?" she asked curiously.

"Oh … I thought I mentioned it to you. We invited the Smiths over for dinner tonight," her mom replied, glancing at her daughter with mild surprise.

The Smiths were Lucas's family, close friends of the Kilanis. The two families had known each other since the Kilanis moved into the neighborhood 19 years ago. The Smiths were their first neighbors to offer a warm welcome. Mr. George Smith and Mrs. Cindy Smith had lived in the area longer and had two sons, Lucas and his younger brother, Charlie.

Mr. Smith was an engineer and Vice President at a biomedical engineering company that specialized in designing and manufacturing medical devices. His job required frequent travel, often leaving Lucas to step up and manage household responsibilities in his father's absence. Recently, Mr. Smith had been posted to Nigeria to help establish a sister company, aiming to improve the availability and distribution of their products across Africa.

Mrs. Cindy Smith was a teacher at an elementary school in Busysville. While she admired her husband's career, she often confided in Klara, Misti's mom, that she disliked the constant travel.

Lucas, the same age as Misti, had been a star quarterback on his school's football team. His good looks, intelligence, and popularity made him a magnet for attention, not only from girls at Swiftly High but also from other schools during matches.

Lucas often found himself in trouble, both at home and at school. His father's frequent absences had a noticeable impact on his behavior despite his popularity and good grades. One particular incident highlighted his tendency to act out.

It happened one afternoon when Lucas was headed to use the boys' restroom. Unfortunately for him, Mr. Lopez, the school janitor, had placed a "Do Not Enter, Cleaning in Progress" sign at the entrance. That restroom was the closest to Lucas's classroom, and not wanting to waste time walking to the second-floor restroom, Lucas decided to push his luck.

When Mr. Lopez spotted him, he firmly but politely instructed Lucas to use the restroom upstairs.

"Hey man, I'm still cleaning. You can't come in here. Please use the restroom on the next floor," Mr. Lopez said.

Lucas, however, refused to comply. "Who are you to tell me what restroom to use, Spanish face?" he snapped, his voice filled with disdain.

Mr. Lopez stood his ground. "All I know is that you can't use this restroom. That's the rule here," he replied firmly.

"Wow … wow … wow," Lucas mocked. "Look who's trying to give orders. Why don't you go back to where you belong? You're not wanted here," he shouted.

Mr. Lopez, visibly offended but composed, responded, "I'll be reporting you to the principal."

"Go f— yourself," Lucas retorted, sticking up his middle finger as he walked away.

It didn't take long before Lucas's name was announced over the loudspeaker, summoning him to the principal's office. When he arrived, Mr. Lopez was already there, waiting. Lucas strolled in as if nothing had happened, refusing to acknowledge Mr. Lopez's presence, his air of indifference masking any guilt or shame.

"Good day, Principal Cheng," Lucas greeted softly, his tone attempting to mask any unease.

"Do you know why you're here this time?" Principal Cheng asked, his voice firm but calm. "This is the second time you've been in my office this week, and the week isn't even over yet."

"I'm confused about why I'm here. What did I do?" Lucas replied, feigning ignorance.

The principal raised an eyebrow. "Let me rephrase. Have you had any encounter with Mr. Lopez today?"

Lucas's face shifted slightly, betraying his pretense. "Oh … that. I didn't do anything wrong. All I told him was that I needed to use the restroom, but he refused to let me," he explained with a grin as if trying to downplay the incident.

"Are you sure that's all that happened?" Principal Cheng pressed. "Because we have cameras everywhere in this building. If I pull up the footage from outside the restroom, will it match your version of events?"

Lucas hesitated, his confidence faltering. "Um … kind of," he admitted reluctantly.

The principal leaned forward, his gaze intense. "Lucas, you're supposed to be a role model—a student others look up to. You're smart, and people admire you. Your mom is a teacher who's making a real difference in children's lives. While she's doing that, you're busy causing headaches for everyone. Why can't you emulate her behavior? When are we going to get a break from your troublemaking? Look at me."

Lucas avoided eye contact, staring at the floor.

"Answer me. Nothing? Crickets? That's what I thought," the principal said, his tone laced with disappointment.

He sighed and continued. "I want you to understand something, Lucas. All of us are from somewhere. No one has the right to tell someone else to 'go back where they belong.' Whether you were born here or not, that kind of attitude has no place in this school—or anywhere else. For your information, Mr. Lopez was born here. The fact that he looks different doesn't make him any less American than you or me."

Principal Cheng straightened in his chair, his tone softening but remaining firm. "Now, I want you to apologize to him. And I mean genuinely."

"… and I will be suspending you for one day. I feel for your mom, who has to deal with this kind of behavior repeatedly. Nevertheless, this school will not tolerate rudeness or disrespect, especially considering the gravity of what you said to Mr. Lopez," Principal Cheng concluded firmly.

Lucas finally turned to face Mr. Lopez. His expression was a mix of guilt and resignation. "I'm sorry," he said quietly, the sincerity in his voice tentative but present.

Mr. Lopez nodded slightly. "Okay, no problem," he responded, his tone measured but kind.

Principal Cheng looked back at Lucas. "I'll be sending an email to your mom about your suspension. You can return to your class now. I trust we are clear on this?"

"Yes, sir," Lucas replied, his shoulders slumping slightly as he turned to leave.

Once Lucas had exited, Principal Cheng sighed and addressed Mr. Lopez. "I apologize for his behavior. I don't know what's gotten into that boy. He comes from a good family."

Mr. Lopez waved off the apology with a small smile. "No worries, Principal. I just didn't want him to treat anyone else that way. That's why I felt the need to report it."

"Thank you for doing so," Principal Cheng said. "It's important we address these issues promptly."

Mr. Lopez stood up, straightening his uniform. "I'll get back to work now."

"All right, have a good day," the principal replied.

"You as well," Mr. Lopez said before leaving the office.

Meanwhile, Lucas returned to his classroom, his steps heavy with lingering embarrassment. Back in the hallway, Mr. Lopez resumed his duties, wheeling his cleaning cart to the next area.

Despite his current role, Mr. Lopez had aspirations beyond his job. At twenty-eight years old, he had a calm maturity about him that stemmed from years of hard work. His parents were immigrants from Spain who had come to the United States in search of better opportunities. His father was a skilled carpenter specializing in custom woodwork, often taking on contracts from both companies and private clients. His mother cleaned houses for some of his father's clients to help make ends meet.

It was from his mother that Mr. Lopez had learned about cleaning. As a high schooler, he often accompanied her to assist with the more labor-intensive tasks. While some of his peers spent weekends at football games or parties, he spent them polishing floors or scrubbing counters, learning the value of diligence and humility. Although his work now might not align with his long-term goals, he carried out his duties with pride and professionalism, always mindful of the foundation his parents had laid for him.

Later, Mr. Lopez attended a trade school to study mechanical engineering. He excelled and secured a well-paying job at a local car manufacturing company in a nearby town. His ultimate dream was to own his own mechanic shop. However, when the company closed due to financial difficulties, his plans unraveled. After years of unsuccessfully searching for a similar job, he returned to the work he knew from his childhood—cleaning. When Swiftly High School posted an opening for a janitor, he applied and got the job. He saw it as a temporary solution while he figured out his next steps.

Back at the Kilanis' house, the family was preparing for the arrival of their guests—the Smiths.

"Mom, is Lucas coming with them?" Misti asked softly.

"I'm not sure. I didn't think it was appropriate to ask, especially after what happened at school yesterday," Klara replied.

"It would probably be hard for him to show up after all that. But if he does, just be yourself. I'm sure he regrets what he did," she added.

"Hopefully. It's going to feel awkward, though," Misti admitted.

"Don't worry, everything will be fine," Klara assured her.

"By the way, where's Milo?" Klara asked.

"He's in his room," Misti replied.

"Please get him for me," Klara said.

Misti went upstairs and knocked on Milo's door.

"Mom wants you downstairs," she said.

"Okay, I'm coming," Milo responded as he followed her down.

"Milo, I need you to clean the bowls in the sink and take out the trash from the kitchen and guest bathroom," his Mom instructed him.

"Sure!" he replied.

The alarm on the cooker went off. Thirty minutes had passed. Misti opened the oven, covered the lasagna pan with a lid, and set it to bake for another twenty minutes as her mom had instructed. Together, Misti and Milo set the table for dinner.

"It's 5:38. I need to take a quick shower; I don't want to smell like food," Klara said to Misti.

"I think I should do the same," Misti replied with a smile.

"Dinner is ready! The Smiths will be here shortly. Everyone better get ready!" Klara called out as she hurried past the living room and up the stairs. Misti followed her, still chatting with her mom.

Chapter Five

It was 6:10. The weather was cooling down, and the evening was growing darker. The day's hustle was gradually winding down, and most businesses in Busysville had already closed for the day. The Kilanis were still in the living room, waiting for their guests. They were watching the popular show *When Life Builds You*, which aired every Friday evening. Most families in Busysville were glued to their TVs at this time, and the streets were nearly empty, with only a few non-local drivers passing through.

The living room was silent, the family fully engrossed in the show. After it ended, Milo broke the quiet.

"I'm starting to get hungry. Are the Smiths coming over still?" he asked, not taking his eyes off the screen.

"Let's give them a little more time," Klara replied.

"They must've gotten caught up with something else. Has George come back yet?" Andy asked, turning to his wife.

"No, not yet. Cindy said he's coming back next month," Klara answered.

"Wow, three months in Africa. Cindy must be having a tough time," Andy said.

"Yes, raising a child alone can't be easy. I don't know how she does it. I don't think I'd be able to manage the way she does. What do you think?" Klara asked.

"I think you'd manage just fine. One thing I've learned is that when you're not in a situation, you think you can't handle it. But when it's your reality, you find a way to cope. It might not be easy, but you'd get through it," Andy reassured her.

"Sometimes, when you leave for just a few days on a medical assignment, I used to feel as if you had been gone for years. Not that I had any big issues with anything, it's just the loneliness … you get what I mean?" Klara told her husband, not really expecting an answer.

"I do. At those times, I used to miss you and the children as well. That's the nature of having a job that requires traveling. We can't escape that part. At least, the travel, in my case, is moderate," Andy Kilani replied, chuckling lightly.

"What was the longest I've been away?" he asked, turning his attention to Klara.

"Two weeks!" Milo chimed in, quick to answer.

"Yeah … those two weeks were … I don't know the right word to describe how those two weeks were in this house," Klara said, looking thoughtfully at her husband.

"I know," Milo responded with a hint of a grin.

"So, how was it for you, son?" Andy asked, now genuinely curious.

"Um … I don't know about Misti … but for me, it meant I didn't have to be bothered about anything … um, that doesn't mean I didn't miss you, but I kind of felt free somehow," Milo stammered, unsure of how to explain it.

"I expected that answer … no surprise there, son," Andy said, a sarcastic tone creeping into his voice.

"I keep an eye on that boy as well to make sure he studies," Klara interjected, glancing at Milo.

"Yeah, but not like I do … he just revealed that," Andy said, glancing at his wife with a smirk.

"Boys will be boys … they don't have to be perfect every time," she replied with a knowing smile, coming to her son's defense.

"Yes … that's what I'm talking about … thanks for having my back, Mom," Milo said, feeling a bit triumphant.

Meanwhile, Misti didn't engage in the conversation her family was having. She was lost in thought, her mind wandering to the dinner with the Smiths that evening. She couldn't shake the feeling that it would be awkward for the first time because of everything that had happened with Lucas. The tension between them was still fresh in her mind, and she couldn't help but wonder how things would unfold.

As the Kilanis continued their discussion, a sudden knock at the door interrupted their conversation – *Knock! Knock! Knock!*

"Milo, go see who is at the door," his dad instructed.

Milo stood up and walked toward the security camera device in the living room, a small touchscreen mounted on the wall. He tapped a few buttons to activate Pinto, the family's artificial intelligence virtual assistant that was linked to the home's security system. Pinto had many features – from controlling the lights and playing music to showing live feeds from the security cameras around the house. Milo used it now to check the front door.

"Mom, it's the delivery guy," he called out after looking at the screen.

"Oh … that must be the delivery of my jewelry," Mrs. Kilani replied, standing up.

She made her way to the door to sign for the package.

"Hello," the delivery guy greeted her as she opened the door.

"Hello," she replied, smiling.

"Can you sign here, please?" the delivery guy asked, holding out his clipboard with a pen.

"Sure," she said as she signed.

After handing the package over, the delivery guy nodded and walked away. Klara closed the door and turned back to her family.

"At first, I thought it was the Smiths," Mr. Kilani said, looking up from the TV, a little disappointed.

"I thought the same, too," Klara agreed, her attention now on the package she had just received. She carefully opened it, revealing her new jewelry.

"Looks beautiful," she said, showing it off to Milo, Misti, and Andy.

"That reminds me," Andy said, breaking the moment of admiration.

"Milo, how were your tests? You had them yesterday, right?" he asked, shifting the focus back to Milo, who was sitting with his arms crossed.

"Yes," Milo answered, though his voice betrayed no excitement or interest in discussing his schoolwork. He was clearly more concerned about the dinner that was still delayed.

"Did you think you did great?" Andy probed, sensing the reluctance in his son's tone.

"Um ... I think so," Milo replied vaguely, his attention clearly elsewhere.

"You think so, or you know so?" his dad pressed further, his voice laced with curiosity.

"Dad, can we just wait for the results to come out first?" Milo said, trying to avoid any more questions. He lowered his head slightly, hoping to end the conversation.

"I tried my best. I left the rest for the teacher. I just don't know if the outcome will be good enough for you and Mom," he added, his sarcasm slipping out as he sunk further into the couch.

"What is up with this 'I left the rest for the teacher' thing?" Mrs. Kilani frowned, clearly frustrated by Milo's dismissive attitude.

"Um … Mom, I thought you were just having my back," Milo said, shrugging his shoulder. "The teacher will decide the scores. I have no control over it."

"There we go again," Mr. Kilani cut in, shaking his head. "Yes, you do have control. If you had studied well and put in your best on those tests, you wouldn't be sitting here saying, "I left the rest for the teacher to decide," he mimicked his son, mocking his careless attitude.

Milo remained silent, unsure of how to respond to his dad's disapproving tone.

"You know this is your last year in middle school, right?" Andy continued. "If you're not taking things seriously now, acting like you don't care, how will you handle things in high school? Tell me," Andy demanded, his voice rising slightly.

"You see your sister?" he continued. "She's won 'Student of the Month' four times in a row this year alone. When are you winning yours?" Mr. Kilani's voice was sharp as he compared Milo to Misti, who had always been the star student.

"I'm being pressured right now," Milo snapped, his voice tinged with frustration. "I thought we were just looking at Mom's jewelry. How did commenting on Mom's jewelry turn into commenting on my tests? I don't want the attention on me this evening," he added, standing up and pacing around the living room to cool off.

"Pressured over what? Your academics?" Mrs. Kilani said with disbelief. "That is no pressure, my dear; it is called accountability and responsibility."

"Children nowadays have everything easy," Mr. Kilani muttered, shaking his head. "Every little thing overwhelms them. I don't know what this generation is turning into."

He paused for a moment, then added, "Back then, life wasn't as easy as it is today. We struggled, but we survived. You see, today, I am a medical doctor, and your mom is a seasoned attorney. We worked hard to be where we are today. It wasn't by chance," he bragged, his chest puffed out a little as he spoke with pride about their accomplishments.

Milo remained quiet, unsure how to respond, as the conversation shifted from his performance to his parents' reflections on their own successes.

"You have food to eat, a roof over your head, social media, technology all around you—games, computers, cell phones, name it! You don't have to go and hawk or work to get this convenient life you have, then you talk about pressure… seriously? … What pressure?" his dad asked, his voice growing more intense as he continued his usual lecture with Milo.

"Plus, you're a guy, my friend," Andy added, his tone firm. "You will have more responsibilities and challenges… so suck it up."

Milo's frustration grew, but he stayed quiet, knowing his dad wasn't about to stop.

"Your dad and I should be talking about pressure, not you," Mrs. Kilani snapped, her eyes narrowing. "You're in eighth grade and talking about pressure? What do you even know about that word? You still have a long way to go in life, and you're complaining already… What?" she asked, her voice sharp and disapproving.

Milo shifted uncomfortably on the couch, his hands folded tightly in his lap. "Dad, you now see why I said what I said before about how I feel any time you're not home… You see? I don't want everything about me to be defined by my test scores at school… At least I'm not failing. What should the parents of those other kids who aren't as smart as I do?" he asked, his voice trailing off as he struggled to express himself.

"All your mom and I want for you is the best in life," Mr. Kilani told him, his tone softening for a moment.

"I know, but I don't think this is the best way to do it," Milo responded quickly. "Dad, you're a doctor… you know what the negative impact of pushing a child too hard is… You guys just need to understand me more," he said, his voice tinged with frustration.

"Dr. Kilani, I understand that you want me to be like you… please let me be me," Milo added, his voice quiet and sad, the weight of his parents' expectations clearly taking a toll on him.

Misti felt sad for her younger brother. She could see how hurt he was, caught in the middle of a conversation that seemed to have no way out. She thought about how to change the subject, but the more she tried to think of something, the more she realized there was nothing easy that would shift the focus. The tension in the room made it hard for her to think of a solution. Just as she was about to say something, the house phone rang.

"Oh … thank goodness!" Misti said silently to herself, feeling a rush of relief. She quickly walked over to pick up the call.

"Phew … saved by the phone," Milo expressed, his voice carrying a hint of humor despite the awkwardness of the situation. He gave a slight grimace, relieved that he wasn't the center of attention anymore.

Misti walked over to the corner of the living room, just before the dining area and the kitchen, where the landline phone was hanging on the wall. She reached for it and answered, trying to sound casual and relaxed.

"Hello … oh … good evening, Mrs. Smith," Misti greeted, trying to mask her relief with politeness.

"Good evening, dear. Is your mom home? Please give the phone to her," Mrs. Smith's voice came through clearly, and Misti quickly relayed the message.

"Yes … Mom, it's Mrs. Smith. She wants to talk to you," Misti called out as she walked the phone over to her mom. She handed the phone to Klara and returned to her spot in the living room, glancing at Milo with a silent look of encouragement.

"Hello Cindy," Mrs. Kilani greeted her friend, her tone warm and friendly.

"Hello Klara, happy weekend!" Cindy replied, sounding upbeat despite her news.

"I am so sorry that we will not be able to make it over today. Charlie has not been feeling okay. He's come down with the flu," Cindy explained apologetically.

"That's fine, I understand," Klara responded, relieved that she and her friend didn't have to address the uncomfortable situation between Misti and Lucas that night, on top of the heated argument she and her husband just had with Milo.

"Um … I want to say that this has nothing to do with what happened between Lucas and Misti. I hope you understand," Cindy clarified, her voice gentle and sincere.

"Lucas still owes Misti an apology. That will happen soon. I hope we haven't caused any inconvenience for not being able to visit today?" Cindy added, sounding genuinely concerned.

"I totally understand," Klara reassured her, wanting to ease her friend's worries.

"Once Charlie feels better, we will pay you a visit," Cindy promised.

"Did you want Andy to visit you instead to examine Charlie?" Klara asked, always thoughtful and wanting to help in any way she could.

"Oh … that will not be necessary, thank you. We had a chat with his primary physician virtually this afternoon. He instructed us already on his treatment," Cindy explained, her tone calm.

"All right then. Give him our warm wishes," Klara said, smiling softly as she glanced at her family, still sitting quietly in the living room.

"I sure will. Thank you for your understanding," Cindy said gratefully.

"I will call you tomorrow to follow up on his condition," Klara added before quickly wrapping up the call.

"Okay, thank you and have a good evening. My greetings to all," Cindy said, sounding like she felt relieved that the misunderstanding had been cleared.

"You as well, bye," Klara said as she hung up the phone.

The call ended, and Klara hung up the phone. She went to the living room to inform her family that the Smiths would not be able to make the visit that day. The call from Cindy saved the night for more drama in talks about Milo.

Chapter Six

It was the last Tuesday in April. The Swiftly Middle School football team—The Tacklers—met on Tuesdays, Thursdays, Fridays, and Saturdays for football practice. The sports locker room was packed with boys either changing into their clothes to shower or relaxing after the day's workout. The room smelled of sweat, perfumes, various body odors, and the fresh scents of soap or shampoo from those who had just cleaned up. Towels, equipment, and water bottles were scattered across the benches and floor. The atmosphere was noisy, with the boys teasing one another.

"Ew! Oh my gosh! Someone just farted! It smells so bad in here," one of the boys exclaimed.

"Ew!" the rest of the boys chorused, covering their noses with their hands.

Mr. Jamal Asad, the football head coach, entered the locker room to relay some information to the team. Mr. Asad had been coaching at Swiftly Middle for about two years. He was well-liked by his students because he consistently strived to help them improve—not only in sports but also in their personal lives. He had discovered that many of the boys on the team did not have a father figure in their lives. Every Saturday, he would personally drive to pick up students from their homes so they could attend football practice at school. These were often students who lacked transportation or could not afford the cost of getting to practice.

In addition to providing transportation, Mr. Asad and his wife supported students who might not be eating enough nutritious food. On some Saturdays, Mrs. Fatimah Asad, his wife, prepared healthy meals for the team. She did this not only to ensure the boys avoided junk food after practice but also to help those who were unsure of where their next meal would come from. Mr. Asad often expressed his gratitude for his wife, proudly sharing how supportive she was of his vision to positively impact the younger generation.

Although the Asads did not have children of their own yet, they treated the team like family. Their dedication and compassion created a sense of belonging and encouragement among the boys, many of whom looked up to Mr. Asad as more than just a coach.

Many times, Mr. Asad had bought groceries for the families of the boys on the team. He often shared with the students that he had grown up poor and, like many of them, did not have a father in his life. Raised by a single mother who struggled to make ends meet for him and his four siblings, he understood the challenges they faced. He recounted how one of his school teachers had seen potential in him and invested both time and money to support him. That teacher not only helped him academically by assisting with homework but also introduced him to sports, especially football, which became a lifelong passion. Mr. Asad emphasized that this experience shaped his desire to give back and help others.

Another way Mr. Asad supported the boys he coached was by organizing camping trips with the help of other coaches. On these trips, he taught the boys practical skills like pitching tents, fishing, and roasting their catch. He even demonstrated the art of building a campfire using the perpendicular layering method, which quickly became a favorite activity. These camping trips served as an opportunity for the boys to bond and strengthen their teamwork. The other coaches divided the boys into groups to teach them respect, responsibility, self-confidence, leadership, and other essential social skills.

During the off-season, Mr. Asad encouraged the boys to participate in volunteer work, especially during the holidays. He often used his bus to transport them to local charitable organizations and food banks, where they helped distribute food to families in need. He believed strongly that helping others was one of the best ways to feel good about oneself and make a meaningful impact. Investing his time and resources in the boys was, to him, a way of ensuring a brighter future. "The support and guidance you receive as a child," he often told them, "can shape not only your life but also the lives of others you touch."

He frequently reminded the boys that he was living proof of this belief. Without the support of his former gym teacher, he said, his life might have turned out very differently, as his family had limited resources to help him succeed. Despite his compassion and leniency with the boys, Mr. Asad maintained high standards of discipline and did not tolerate bad behavior.

"Hey ... guys ... tone it down. It's way too loud in here," Mr. Asad said, raising his voice to be heard over the noise.

Then, catching a whiff of the air, he jokingly added, "Do we have a dead rat in here?" while pretending to catch his breath. His humor broke through the noise, and the boys erupted into laughter, the camaraderie filling the room.

"Someone farted!" one of the boys shouted, prompting laughter from the others.

"Oh ... okay. I have an announcement to make," Mr. Asad said, raising his voice slightly to regain their attention.

"Remember, for Thursday's football practice, you will need to wear full training gear. Make sure to come early and be on your best behavior," he continued firmly.

"I've been informed that some of you were acting disrespectfully toward your teammates before today's practice. I will not tolerate any unruly behavior—there is no room for hate here. You are a team. You are one," he emphasized.

"I'll also be sending an email to your parents about today's behavior as a reminder to keep up with our team standards. And don't forget, there's a fundraiser for the upcoming New Jersey game next week," he added.

"By the way, today's practice was great. Keep it up, and continue improving! See you all Thursday."

"Thanks, Coach!" the boys responded in unison.

Mr. Asad smiled and walked away, leaving the boys to resume their chatting, teasing, and playing as they changed to go home.

"Mr. Asad is the reason I'm still playing football. Otherwise, I would have quit a long time ago," Caleb said to Milo as they walked out of the training facility.

"Me too," Milo agreed.

"I can't wait to graduate from this school, but I'm going to miss Mr. Asad a lot," Caleb admitted.

"Same here. I don't think I'm going to play football in high school, though. But I haven't gotten the courage to tell my dad yet," Milo said, chuckling nervously.

"He's going to be really disappointed," Caleb replied with a smirk.

"So, have your parents figured out you're serious about not playing football in high school?" Milo asked.

"Yeah, but they didn't take me seriously. They think I'm joking. But I'm not, Milo. I want to be a man of my own dreams, not theirs," Caleb said, jabbing a finger into his chest for emphasis.

"It's like all parents go to some secret school together. They think alike, act alike," Milo joked, laughing.

"They want their sons and daughters to play sports, join extracurriculars, and still get straight A's—or worse, be like someone else's kid," Caleb added with an exasperated shrug.

"I know! It's a lot to handle just so they can feel like we fit in," Milo said sarcastically.

"I feel you, bruh," Caleb replied.

"And don't get me started on teachers like Mr. Gold, who assign piles of homework every single day," Milo groaned.

"You're right! It's like that dude has nothing better to do than give us more work to take home. He's singlehandedly making English Language Arts the most boring class ever. Doesn't he get tired of marking all that homework? Doesn't he have a life outside school?" Caleb asked, clearly not expecting an answer.

The boys laughed together, their frustrations temporarily eased as they walked toward home, carrying their shared dreams and struggles like teammates on the field.

"I wonder how that guy relaxes. He doesn't care that we have other stuff to do or other classes to study for. Remember the other time he gave us, like, forty vocabulary words to study—for a test he scheduled just two days later? Caleb, you remember that test, right? Who does that?" Milo complained.

"Of course I do. Who could forget? It's the one he emailed our parents about because we all failed. Ridiculous! I don't think the dude has kids yet. He doesn't understand how stressful it is to grow up in this age," Caleb said, laughing.

"No, he doesn't—just like some other adults," Milo agreed.

"I remember sitting down for that test, and my mind just went blank. I had forgotten the meanings of most of the words because there were way too many to study in the little time he gave us. Why do some teachers do that?" Caleb asked, laughing even harder.

"Yeah, I felt the same way. It's like they're setting us up to fail. You feel helpless, right?" Milo asked.

"Exactly! And now we've got another assignment from him due tomorrow. Plus, there's the Art presentation and the Math exam tomorrow, too. It's going to be a busy day," Caleb pointed out.

"Don't worry, we'll survive, like we always do," Milo said, trying to reassure his friend.

"I hope so," Caleb replied.

"And what's up with the new Math curriculum they're introducing next year—Prekan Math, or whatever they're calling it? I'm just glad I'll be out of here by then," Caleb added.

"Right? I've got a friend at another school who's already taking it. He says it's the most confusing and frustrating Math class he's ever had. It's all about proving your answers, like explaining *why* an answer is what it is. Oh boy," Milo said, shaking his head.

"I hope they stick with the Math everyone actually understands. Why cause more headaches for students? Oh man," Caleb said, exasperated.

As they continued talking, one of their teammates, Rye, came running up behind them.

"Hey, man! You left your jacket on the bench!" Rye called out to Caleb.

"Oh, thanks! Dang, I didn't even realize I wasn't holding it," Caleb said, taking the jacket. "Thanks, bruh," he added with a grin.

"No worries," Rye replied.

"You're lucky. I lost my sneakers last week. Someone took them from under the bench while I went to the bathroom. By the time I came back, they were gone," Milo said, shaking his head.

"Wow. Lucky me indeed!" Caleb said, laughing.

The three boys laughed together for a moment before eventually heading their separate ways, their camaraderie lingering as a reminder of the friendships that made their hectic school lives more bearable.

Chapter Seven

At the Kilanis', Misti was in her room, scrolling through social media. She was watching various how-to videos on beauty, hoping to learn tips for dressing up for the prom and graduation parties planned for the seniors of Swiftly High School. After a while, she walked over to her mirror to examine her face and body.

"I wish I had a slimmer body like the model in that LooksTube video. I think I need to lose more weight," she muttered to herself.

"Ugh! My forehead is too flat for this short hair. I wish my hair were longer. Maybe I need a headband to cover up part of my forehead. I don't want others laughing at me like they usually do," she said, her voice tinged with worry.

"… And my eyebrows—too thin. I think I need to order that eyebrow gel I saw earlier. Maybe it'll make mine as thick as the girl's in the video," she thought.

Determined, she went back to some of the beauty tutorials she had watched earlier, searching for the specific video featuring the gel. After finding it, she placed an order. Feeling a small sense of accomplishment, she returned to the mirror, this time leaning in closer to scrutinize her reflection. She took a few selfies, talking to herself as she envisioned how she would look for the upcoming events.

Walking over to her closet, she began testing out different dresses with matching shoes.

"I wore this to the homecoming party last year. I don't want to wear it again—especially not to school," she thought, pulling out a dress and holding it up. "I looked great in it last time, but I don't want people to think I don't have other clothes."

She glanced at the three new dresses her mom had recently bought for her. Unsure which one to choose for prom, she hesitated, lost in thought. Suddenly, there was a knock at the door—Knock! Knock! Knock!

"Coming!" Misti shouted, dashing to the door. She had been expecting her friend, Elise. As she hurried downstairs, Slotty ran alongside her, wagging her tail excitedly.

"Hey, girlfriend!" Misti greeted Elise, opening the door.

"Hi, Misti!" Elise replied.

"Hey there, cutie!" Elise cooed at Slotty, crouching to rub her back affectionately. The dog responded with enthusiastic tail wags as both friends headed upstairs to Misti's room.

"I've been getting ready for prom and the graduation parties," Misti told Elise as they entered the room.

"Me too! I just bought a pair of high heels. I don't want to look too short in my dress. I wish I were a little taller," Elise said with a hint of sadness.

"I bought Clearons face moisturizer from LooksTube. I've been using it for two days now, and I hope it clears up the acne on my face like it's advertised to," Elise said, her voice tinged with worry as she looked in the mirror. "I just don't want to give Lindsey and Claire another chance to pick on me," she added with a sigh.

"Wow! I just ordered an eyebrow gel from LooksTube right before you arrived," Misti said excitedly, showing her friend a picture of the product on her laptop.

"I don't want to look like a nerd either," Misti continued, gesturing as she spoke. "I'm definitely not wearing my prescription glasses. I'll wear my contact lenses instead, even though they sometimes irritate my eyes. It's worth the pain to avoid being made fun of."

"Sometimes, I wish I looked more like my dad," Elise said, jumping into the conversation. "At least I'd be taller and have his pointed nose instead of being short with this big, flat nose like Mom's," she added, touching her nose and laughing. "Or maybe just a little bigger. I feel like I'm way too thin," she said, glancing at her reflection again.

"If Clearons works for you, maybe I'll try it too," Misti teased, grinning at her friend.

"You barely have any acne. Why would you need Clearons?" Elise asked, raising an eyebrow.

"You said *barely*, which means I have at least a teeny tiny bit … duh!" Misti replied, both of them bursting into laughter.

"It's that *teeny tiny* bit I want to get rid of," she added, shaking her head as she moved toward her closet.

Misti returned her attention to the three new dresses hanging neatly in her closet. She carefully considered which one would be perfect for the upcoming prom and graduation parties. Elise joined her, offering ideas for pairing dresses with accessories and shoes. Their laughter and chatter filled the room as they debated styles and colors.

Suddenly, they heard footsteps approaching. Curious, Misti walked to the door and opened it to see who it was. Since Elise's arrival, the only other presence in the house had been Slotty, the family dog.

"Oh, it's my mom! She got home early today. I thought it might be Milo," Misti said to Elise as she peered out the door. "I'll be right back," she added, leaving the room to meet her mom.

Elise stayed behind, listening to the faint sound of Misti and her mother chatting in the distance. Slotty trotted into the room, curling up next to Elise on the floor. She rubbed her neck and back affectionately before lying back on Misti's bed. Slotty shifted closer as though she were keeping watch over her.

A few minutes later, Misti returned, holding a plate of chocolate cookies and a cup of strawberry juice. "Snack time!" she announced cheerfully, placing the treats on the bedside table.

"Sorry for keeping you waiting," Misti apologized to her friend, handing her some cookies and juice.

"No worries. I overheard you chatting with your mom … I wish I could talk with mine the same way," Elise lamented, taking a bite of the cookie.

"Mm … mm, these are so delicious. Did you bake them?" she asked, her tone lightening.

"My mom did," Misti replied.

"Nice … so you also have a mom baking you cookies? Wow, you're living the dream," Elise teased.

"I bake most of the ones you eat whenever you visit, but these ones are hers," Misti said with a small smile.

"Mm … I can taste the difference," Elise replied, smiling back.

"My mom is either too tired or too busy to bake because of the nature of her job. Honestly, sometimes, it can be exhausting dealing with both my parents, especially when they come back from work. Most times, I just pretend to be asleep to avoid their drama," Elise admitted, her tone turning somber.

"You're kidding, right?" Misti asked, clearly surprised.

"No, I'm not. I don't like talking about it, but I told you because you're my best friend," Elise said softly.

"You know we tell each other everything. How come you never mentioned this before? Listen, my parents, though they're loving and caring, can also be demanding, especially with Milo. I always feel bad for him," Misti confessed.

"So, we all have silent pressures we're dealing with. Don't think you're the only young person in the world with problems. I have mine too, even if the situations are different," she added, moving closer to Elise for emphasis.

"I've learned to voice my frustrations with my parents. After all, I'm an adult now—we're eighteen, Elise," Misti continued, tapping her friend on the shoulder.

Elise sighed. "They have so much stress from work, especially my dad. He comes home and takes it out on my younger sisters and me. Sometimes, even my mom isn't spared," she finally opened up.

"Imagine two people coming home wounded from work—maybe by their boss, colleagues, or just the workload—then unleashing all that pain and stress on their own family for the slightest mistake, or sometimes for no reason at all," Elise described, her voice thick with emotion.

"My sisters and I are always walking on eggshells when both of them are home. We can't afford to add more pressure to ourselves—on top of school stress and our personal struggles. Parents don't realize that we face our own demons too.

We have our own problems!" she emphasized, her voice trembling.

"I feel for you," Misti said gently, placing a comforting hand on Elise's shoulder.

"The worst is when they both unload their stress on each other after work. Oh my … it's not pretty at all. They argue, yell, and shout at the top of their lungs. It's heartbreaking to watch, and it's taking a mental toll on all of us," Elise continued, her voice heavy with frustration.

"One time, I told them they should look for different jobs because their current ones were tearing us apart at home. Guess what? They both said it's not easy to find another job. So, I guess we're stuck in this mess," she said with a resigned shrug.

"Do they work at the same place?" Misti asked curiously.

"Oh … no. They're just unlucky enough to be working at terrible places. Or maybe it's bad bosses, bad colleagues, or bad environments … who knows? It's almost funny how both my parents can work at different companies and still have such similar problems. It's tough!" Elise explained, shaking her head.

"Don't worry; you'll be free soon," Misti said encouragingly, offering her a reassuring smile.

"Yep! I can't wait to go to college. That will be my escape. I just feel bad for the twins—they'll be stuck with this chaos for another two years if things don't change," Elise said, a tinge of sadness in her voice.

"You see why I come here so often? It's to escape the drama. It's so much more peaceful here," she added with a small laugh. "You're lucky, Misti … truly blessed." She glanced at the clock on the wall.

It was 6:29 p.m. Elise walked over to the window and peered outside. The daylight was fading quickly, the sky dimming as the evening surrendered to night.

"It's getting dark! I better get going, Misti," she said, her tone tinged with concern.

"Oh … okay," Misti replied, sensing the worry in her friend's voice. "Everything will be all right. Just pray and read your Bible. Remember, God is always there for you," she added with a warm, encouraging smile.

"I will. Wish me some luck," Elise said, managing a small grin.

"See ya!" Misti said as she waved.

"See ya!" Elise replied playfully, trying to lift her own spirits.

Misti walked her friend to the front door, watching as she stepped into the twilight. As Elise disappeared down the path, Misti sighed, feeling grateful for her own home life but also deeply concerned for her friend's struggles.

Chapter Eight

The clouds appeared dark and thick, and the wind was blowing heavily. The sounds of objects clashing and banging on the streets echoed as the wind swept them along. The streets looked surprisingly cleaner as the wind blew papers and other debris away. Suddenly, it started to rain—heavy, torrential rain. A loud pounding could be heard as raindrops hit the roofs, and the streets were soaked in a matter of minutes.

Some people struggled to keep their umbrellas from being blown away by the force of the wind, while others, who didn't have umbrellas, were drenched to the skin. Drivers honked their horns in frustration as traffic crawled at a slow pace. Some drivers attempted to overtake others in a rush to get to their destinations. The heavy rain caused significant traffic delays, as fallen trees blocked roads in some areas, either slowing traffic or creating complete roadblocks. The police and firefighters were seen handling the situation, clearing fallen trees from the roads or manually directing traffic, since some of the traffic lights had stopped working due to the pounding rain and wind. The floods made the situation worse for the firefighters, preventing them from reaching certain areas.

Misti looked out the window from her room and saw that the stop sign at the T-junction on their street had been bent downward. She also noticed that the tree in front of their neighbor's house across the street had split in half, with one part lying on the grass beneath it. The mailbox in front of the Kilani's house had not been spared either—it had fallen off its stand and landed on their driveway.

Their TV was tuned to the local channel, KWYM 3, where they were monitoring updates on the devastation caused by the storm. The breaking news showed images of people packed into train stations and the post office, taking cover from the rain. Misti and Milo began to worry that their parents might be trapped somewhere, whether at work or stuck in traffic. Milo went to Misti's room to ask if their parents had contacted her, but she told him she had not heard from them yet.

After about two hours, the rain finally stopped, and the sky cleared as if nothing had happened. The clouds parted, and the chaos of the storm seemed a distant memory, though the minor devastation was still visible everywhere. Traffic slowly began to move again as the floods began to recede. Within a short time, things started to return to normal.

"Ring! Ring! Ring!" The house phone at the Kilanis' rang. Milo walked over to pick it up.

"Hello, who am I speaking with?" he asked.

"Hello, Milo! How are you doing? It's Mrs. Smith," came the voice on the other end.

"Oh… hello, Mrs. Smith. I'm doing well," Milo replied.

"Is Charlie feeling better?" he asked.

"Yes, he is. Thanks for asking. He's getting his strength back and is able to eat and play again," Mrs. Smith said.

"That's great to hear! Have you heard from Mr. Smith?" Milo inquired.

"Yes, he should be back in the U.S. soon. Thanks for asking. By the way, is your mom home?" Mrs. Smith asked.

"No, she's not. She hasn't come back from work yet," Milo replied.

"I tried calling her cell phone but couldn't reach her, so I thought I'd try the house phone. The rainstorm must have caused some delays, either on the road or at work," Mrs. Smith explained.

"I'll try her cell phone again. If I can't get through, I'll leave her a message to let her know that Lucas and I will be over this evening. Hopefully, the roads will be clear by then," she added.

"Alright," Milo said.

"Okay, bye for now. See you this evening, hopefully," Mrs. Smith said.

"Okay, bye, Mrs. Smith," Milo replied, and the call ended.

Milo went back to his bedroom to continue playing his video game. His room was adjacent to the bathroom down the first-floor hallway. The walls were painted sky blue, and one wall featured football-themed decals above his bed. In the corner of his room, there was a table and chair where his gaming setup was. On either side of his bed were two lampstands. The floor was covered with carpet.

Suddenly, the house phone rang again—"Ring! Ring! Ring!" Milo hurried downstairs to pick it up.

"Hello, who's calling?" he asked.

"Hello, this is Dr. Robert from St. Peter's Hospital. Is this the Kilanis' residence?" the doctor asked.

"Yes, it is. How can I help you?" Milo responded, thinking the doctor might be a colleague of his dad's.

"Is there an adult I can speak with?" the doctor asked.

"Yes, my sister. Is everything alright?" Milo asked anxiously.

"I wasn't able to reach your dad on his cell, so I decided to call this number," the doctor explained.

"He's at work. He's a doctor too, so he might be busy attending to patients or stuck in traffic," Milo said, wondering what the call could be about.

"Alright, let me speak with your sister," the doctor said.

"Sure, please hold on while I get her," Milo replied.

Milo ran to get Misti. She was in her bedroom, studying for her upcoming Chemistry exam, which was scheduled for the following morning. He quickly told Misti about the doctor's call and that he wanted to speak with her. They both went downstairs to the landline phone. Misti picked it up, and Milo waited anxiously, hoping to hear why the doctor had called.

"Hello?" Misti answered, her voice filled with anticipation.

"Hello, this is Dr. Robert from St. Peter's Hospital," he introduced himself.

"I'm calling to inform you that your mom was involved in a motor accident. I wasn't able to reach your dad, so I decided to call this number," the doctor said gently.

"Oh my goodness! Oh my goodness!" Misti repeated, her voice trembling.

It felt as though her entire world had just collapsed. Her heartbeat raced, her hands shook, and her stomach twisted into knots. Her eyes widened in shock, and for a moment, she was speechless, frozen in place.

Milo rushed to her side, panicking. "Misti! Misti! What's going on? What's happening?" he asked urgently, his voice filled with concern.

"Hello… are you still there?" the doctor asked, noticing the silence on the other end of the line.

"Are you two okay?" he asked, his voice concerned.

"I… I'm not sure," Misti eventually replied, her voice shaky and confused.

"You don't need to come to the hospital right away. The roads are still bad. I recommend you wait for your dad to return before taking any action," the doctor advised calmly.

"We just wanted to inform you that Mrs. Kilani is in critical condition but in good hands. Again, you don't need to come immediately," he reassured her.

"Thank you, doctor… I'll be fine. I'll head over soon. The hospital isn't far from here, and it looks like the rain has stopped. The weather's clearing up," Misti replied, her voice still unsteady but trying to sound more composed.

"All right… please come to the trauma unit waiting room and check in with the receptionist. It's on the first floor," he instructed.

"Take it easy and be safe out there. See you soon," he added kindly.

"Okay… thank you, doctor," Misti replied, her voice heavy with sadness as she hung up the phone.

The call ended. Misti quickly recounted to Milo what the doctor had said. She called her dad, but he was unreachable. Then, she tried calling his office, and the receptionist informed her that he had already left for the day. Misti told Milo to stay behind and update their dad once he got home.

She explained that she would be leaving for the hospital. St. Peter's Hospital, one of the major medical centers in Busysville, was about a sixteen-minute walk from their home.

It was half past five. About an hour after Misti left for the hospital, the front doorbell rang. Milo checked the security camera to see who it was. It was Mrs. Smith and Lucas. She had called earlier to say she would visit that evening, though she hadn't known about the accident yet. Milo went to open the door for them.

"Hello, Milo! I went to the pharmacy nearby to pick up some medicine for Charlie, so I thought I'd stop by now to save myself another trip," Mrs. Smith said, entering with Lucas and Charlie. "Is your mom home?"

"Good evening, Mrs. Smith. Hey, Lucas, hey Charlie. No, she's not home," Milo replied sadly.

"Huh, I thought she'd be back by now. That's why I decided to come by," Mrs. Smith said, looking puzzled.

"What's wrong? You sound upset," she observed, noticing Milo's downcast expression.

"Misti just left for the hospital... Mom was in a car accident on her way home from work. She's been admitted to St. Peter's Hospital in the trauma unit," Milo explained.

"What? A car accident?" Mrs. Smith exclaimed. "You said St. Peter's Hospital? Trauma unit? Do you know what caused the accident?"

"We don't know the details yet," Milo replied.

"Maybe the weather had something to do with it... I'll head over there now," Mrs. Smith said, her voice shaky.

"We can't reach Dad. His phone isn't working or something. It's very unlike him to not call back after a missed call..." Milo trailed off, feeling anxious.

"You stay here," Mrs. Smith advised. "And don't worry, everything will be fine. Your mom will be home before you know it," she reassured him as she prepared to leave for the hospital.

"It's okay, man," Lucas said quietly to Milo, offering a faint smile.

"See you later," Mrs. Smith called as she left with her sons.

Chapter Nine

St. Peter's Hospital was a huge, newly built, state-of-the-art medical facility in Busysville. The hospital had been constructed as part of an expansion of the St. Peter's group of hospitals to cater to the health needs of Busysvillians and the neighboring cities. With a 121-bed capacity, it offered acute care services. The two-story medical building was well-equipped, with rooms, wards, and various departments. The first floor housed waiting rooms, patient rooms, and treatment rooms, while the second floor was designated for administrative offices, maintenance areas, a technology/control room, and changing rooms for health workers, among other facilities.

Misti arrived at the hospital without much stress despite the unfavorable weather. She only had to deal with muddy grounds, which made her walk a little challenging. Fortunately, the short distance from her home to the hospital made it manageable. For those arriving by car, navigating the roads would have been tougher, as some streets remained closed despite the town's quick recovery to normalcy.

As she approached the hospital entrance, Misti noticed a scraper mat placed at the doorway. Its purpose was to remove mud or other debris from the soles of visitors' shoes before they entered the building. The scraper mat was a practical addition, as the rain had left many with muddy footwear. Misti diligently cleaned her sneakers on the mat, ensuring she wouldn't leave tracks inside. Cleaners were also stationed throughout the hospital, constantly mopping the floors to maintain cleanliness.

Reaching the reception area, Misti approached the desk where a medical receptionist was seated.

"Good day. I'm Misti Kilani. I'm here for my mom, Mrs. Kilani. She was brought here today after an accident. Dr. Robert called my family to inform us about the incident, which is why I'm here," Misti explained.

"Okay … let me check my records," the receptionist replied, turning to her computer.

"Sorry, could you repeat the last name?"

"Kilani. Do you need me to spell it?" Misti asked, leaning forward slightly.

"No need, thank you … just a moment … oh, I found her. She's been admitted. You can take a seat; the doctor will be out shortly to speak with you," the receptionist said with a polite smile.

"All right, thank you."

Misti moved to the seating area, where other visitors were waiting. As she settled into her seat, she noticed a pen had fallen to the floor nearby. A young man around her age seemed to have dropped it.

"Hello … I think you dropped your pen," Misti called out to him, extending the pen in his direction. The boy looked up, slightly startled, before smiling and taking it from her.

"Thanks," he said quietly, glancing at her before returning his attention to the magazine in his lap.

Misti sat back in her chair, waiting for the doctor to arrive with news of her mother's condition.

The boy then returned to the medical receptionist, handing her the patient intake form he had just completed for his mom. As he came back, he sat down beside Misti.

"Hey, thanks again for earlier. I'm Jack. What brought you here?" he asked.

"My mom. She had a motor accident," Misti replied.

"Oh … that's serious. I hope she gets better soon," he said with concern.

"I hope so, too. I'm still waiting for the doctor to give me more updates. Earlier, he told me her condition was critical," she explained.

"I'm really sorry to hear that. I hope everything turns out okay," he encouraged.

"… and what about you? What brought you here?" Misti asked in return.

"In my case, it's also my mom … but not because of an accident. She got burned. She accidentally set herself on fire with her cigarette," he shared.

"How did that happen?" Misti asked, intrigued but cautious.

"She was drunk," Jack began. "She threw her lit cigarette onto the couch she was sitting on, and it caught fire. Before she realized it, the flames spread to her clothes. She was badly burned. She nearly burned the house down. Thank God I was home; otherwise, it could've ended much worse," he explained.

Misti listened intently, and Jack continued.

"She's an alcoholic. Ever since my dad left us, she's turned to alcohol to cope. Her drinking has spiraled out of control. She's lost all her savings, fallen behind on bills, recently lost her job, and now the bank is about to evict us from our home," he said, his voice heavy with frustration.

"I'm sorry for unloading all of this on you," he added, glancing at her apologetically. "I know it's selfish of me to vent to someone I just met. It's just that … sometimes I really need someone to talk to. I'm an only child, and I don't have close family or friends to lean on."

"It's no bother at all," Misti said, her voice warm and empathetic.

"You know, sometimes we think we're the only ones going through pain," she added gently. "But when we hear others share their stories, it makes us grateful for what we have."

"You're right," Jack admitted, though his expression remained clouded. "But it's so hard. Most of the time, she passes out from drinking. I'm the one who has to deal with everything—the bills, taking care of her, even working part-time to make ends meet. I've had to skip school so many times just to stay home with her," he said.

Misti nodded, silently urging him to continue.

"The worst part is," Jack went on, "after she recovers, she just starts drinking all over again. It's a cycle that never ends. Sometimes … sometimes I feel like running away," he confessed, his voice breaking slightly.

"… but I've decided not to do that. If I should leave, believe it or not, it won't be long before something bad and irreversible happens to her, and no one will be around to help. That's why I've chosen to stay," Jack added.

"Wow … I respect your courage," Misti said sincerely.

"Do you guys live around here?" she asked.

"No, we live in Herostown. She was transferred here from another hospital because her burns are severe," Jack explained.

"My dad works in Herostown. He's a medical doctor at St. Mary's Hospital," Misti told him.

"Really? I know St. Mary's! That's where she was first taken. When the doctors there saw that her burns were beyond what they could handle, they transferred her here," he said.

"Wow, that's tough," Misti responded sympathetically.

As they continued their conversation, the medical receptionist called Jack's name. He and Misti exchanged good luck wishes before he left to speak with the receptionist. She directed him to the room where his mom was being treated.

"Misti Kilani?" the receptionist called out.

Misti turned, spotting the doctor standing near the workstation where the receptionist was seated. She walked over and was directed to meet the doctor in a nearby room adjacent to the waiting area.

Inside, the doctor greeted her and explained that her mom was in critical condition but that the medical team had things under control.

"I'll need to discuss her situation in more detail with your dad when he arrives," the doctor concluded.

After their brief conversation, Misti returned to her seat in the waiting room. She sat quietly, glancing occasionally at the clock as she waited for her dad to arrive.

A few minutes later, Mrs. Smith and Lucas arrived and found Misti sitting in the trauma unit's waiting room. She was watching TV, trying to distract herself from worrying about her mom. The waiting room had an open layout, with chairs arranged neatly in two layers facing the central area where the receptionist attended to visitors. The walls were painted a sterile white, decorated with a few serene artworks. Modest but bright lighting illuminated the room, creating a calm atmosphere. A TV mounted in the corner played softly while a water dispenser stood at the opposite end near two stools stacked with assorted magazines.

"Misti, how are you holding up?" a familiar voice asked.

Startled, Misti turned to see Mrs. Smith.

"Hello, Mrs. Smith … um," she replied, surprised to see her at the hospital.

"Milo told me about what happened, so I decided to come," Mrs. Smith explained kindly.

"Oh … thanks for coming. My mom is in critical condition … the doctor told me," Misti informed them sadly.

"Oh God!" Mrs. Smith exclaimed, her face filled with concern.

"Hello, Misti," Lucas greeted her, his tone sober and apologetic.

"Hi, Lucas … thanks for coming," Misti said softly.

"Have you been able to reach your dad?" Mrs. Smith asked.

"Fortunately, yes. He just called me right before you arrived. He lost his cell phone, and that's why we couldn't reach him. He didn't know about the situation until he got home, and Milo had to explain everything to him. He's on his way here now. He should be here soon," Misti explained, her voice calm but tinged with exhaustion.

As Misti spoke to Mrs. Smith, Mr. Kilani entered the waiting room, his face etched with worry and anxiety. Still dressed in his work outfit, he hurriedly walked up to where Misti was sitting.

"Ladybug … I hope you're alright?" he asked gently as he hugged her tightly.

"Hello, Dad. She's in room 112. The doctor said she's in critical condition and that no visitors are allowed to see her yet," Misti explained quickly, trying to keep her emotions in check.

"Thank you for being here, Mrs. Smith … and you too, Lucas and Charlie. Your presence means so much to us," he said, his gratitude evident.

"I hope you're feeling better, Charlie. I'm sorry that your mom had to bring you here under these circumstances," he added kindly.

"… and I'm so sorry no one could reach me earlier. It's just … it's unfortunate that the one day I needed to be available was the day I wasn't reachable. I feel so guilty," he lamented, his voice heavy with regret.

He then walked to the medical receptionist to introduce himself and inquire about his wife.

"Good evening, Miss. I'm Dr. Kilani. My wife is a patient here," he said.

"Oh … good evening, Doctor. I'll notify the attending physician that you're here. Everything will be alright. Please take a seat," the receptionist reassured him with a warm smile.

"Thank you," he replied before returning to his seat.

Lucas leaned toward Misti and asked, "Do you want to go get some snacks with me from the vending machine?"

She nodded. "Sure, why not."

As they walked to the vending machine, Lucas broke the silence. "I'm truly sorry for what I did to you at school the other day. My mom and I went to your house to apologize, but when Milo told us about your mom's situation, we came straight here instead. I know this isn't the place to talk about it, but I just …," he stuttered, struggling to find the right words.

"I understand. I forgive you," Misti cut in softly, sparing him from further fumbling.

"I appreciate the fact that you and your mom came here. You both did not let me feel alone before my dad got here," Misti added sincerely.

"By the way … we have the Chemistry test tomorrow," Misti reminded him as they walked back.

"Yeah, I did prepare for it … did you?" Lucas asked, trying to shift the conversation to something lighter.

"I was studying when Dr. Robert called about my mom … I should be fine," she replied, her confidence steady despite the circumstances.

When they returned to the waiting area with their snacks, Dr. Kilani was deep in conversation with Dr. Robert. Mrs. Smith was flipping through magazines on the small stools nearby. She glanced up and spotted Misti and Lucas approaching.

"Hey, guys, are you all right?" Mrs. Smith asked, her voice warm with concern.

"Yes, Mrs. Smith!" Misti replied, nodding.

"Yes, Mom!" Lucas said at the same time as Misti, his response earning a small smile from her.

Dr. Kilani joined them soon after wrapping up his conversation with Dr. Robert. The small group—Misti, Lucas, and Mrs. Smith—listened attentively as he updated them on Mrs. Klara Kilani's condition.

"How is Mom doing now?" Misti asked, her voice trembling slightly.

"The doctor just informed me that her condition has moved from critical to stable … thank God!" Dr. Kilani announced, relief visible on his face.

"Oh … thank goodness!" Mrs. Smith exclaimed, echoing his sentiment.

"She'll stay admitted until her condition improves. We won't be able to see her until the doctor gives permission. So, I'll stay here overnight," he explained.

"Misti, you can go with Mrs. Smith to get a ride home. Let Milo know that everything is fine. I'll try and get a new phone tomorrow when I take a break from here," he instructed gently.

"All right, Dad," Misti replied, nodding obediently.

"Focus on your test tomorrow. Your mom will be okay," he encouraged her with a reassuring smile.

"Thanks again for coming, Mrs. Smith and Lucas. It really means a lot," he said, expressing his gratitude.

"Our pleasure!" Mrs. Smith responded warmly.

"I'll visit when she gets better. I hope I can see her then," Mrs. Smith added.

"Good night, Dr. Kilani," Lucas said politely.

"Good night, Lucas," Dr. Kilani replied, appreciating the boy's sincerity.

Misti left with Mrs. Smith, Charlie, and Lucas, and the quartet made their way back home. Dr. Andy Kilani remained at the hospital, settling in to spend the night in the waiting room. He watched the ebb and flow of patients and visitors entering and leaving the hospital, their movements filling the quiet space with muted activity. Outside, the night had grown darker and cooler, a peaceful contrast to the hospital's steady hum of life.

Chapter Ten

It had been four days since Mrs. Kilani was admitted to the hospital. Her family made sure to visit regularly, ensuring they were there whenever she was stable enough to receive visitors. Their community had rallied around them, offering immense support during this challenging time. Friends from work, church, and the neighborhood had been particularly helpful. Mrs. Smith ensured that the Kilani children had homemade dinners every evening while their mom was away. Families dropped off groceries, and others stopped by the house just to say hello and remind them that they were not alone.

The Kilani family's reputation for helping others had made them beloved in the community. Every year, Mr. Kilani and his team of doctors organized health fairs and medical screenings for people without health insurance in Busysville. These events included services like eye exams, oral health checkups, and flu vaccinations, all offered at no charge. Free promotional health kits were also handed out to participants. During Thanksgiving, the family sponsored the local Thanksgiving Food and Toy Drive for those in need. It was this consistent generosity that spurred the overwhelming support they now received. People believed that one good turn deserved another, and the Kilanis were proof of that.

As the new day began, its brightness brought a glimpse of hope for the family. The sun was just rising, and life in Busysville was already bustling. Misti and Milo were preparing for school when they heard their father come home from the hospital. Since his wife's admission, Dr. Kilani had developed a routine: he stayed overnight at the hospital, returned home each morning to freshen up, dressed for work, and repeated the cycle. It had been an exhausting four days for him, but his dedication never wavered.

"Good morning, Dad," Misti and Milo greeted him in unison.

"Good morning, darlings," he replied with a tired but warm smile.

"I hope you both had a good night's rest," he added, his voice full of concern.

"Kind of …," Misti answered, her tone reflective.

"Not too bad," Milo chimed in, shrugging slightly.

"Were you able to talk to Mom yet?" Milo asked, his face filled with anticipation.

"Not yet," their father replied gently. "She's been sleeping and resting. She did open her eyes and saw me, but she didn't have the strength to talk yet. She just nodded her head. Let's give her some more time," he encouraged them.

"Don't worry, your mom is going to be fine," he added with determination. "I came home to freshen up before heading to work."

"Did you make breakfast?" he asked, turning his attention to Misti.

"Yes, Daddy. I made some scrambled eggs and sausage. There's some left in the pan," she told him, her tone brightening at the small contribution.

"You both should focus on what you need to get done at school. Leave the worry about your mom to me. She will be okay … Dr. Robert has assured me. Worrying about the situation will not solve anything; it will only affect you. I don't want you to use this as an excuse not to do what you are expected to do well. You heard me right," he affirmed, his tone firm but reassuring.

"Okay," they both replied, nodding in agreement.

"Everything will be all right," Andy assured them again, his voice carrying an air of finality. "Now hasten up so you don't get late for school. We'll talk when you get back, and I'll let you know if it would be necessary for both of you to come see your mom today. That will depend on the doctor's decision," he expressed with calm authority.

"Understood," Milo said, speaking for them both as he grabbed his school bag.

With that, Milo and Misti left for school while their dad prepared for work. Dr. Andy Kilani was a well-known medical doctor with a reputation for excellence in treating and caring for families. As a general practitioner, he was celebrated for his groundbreaking work and research in family health, earning numerous awards for his dedication and innovative approaches. Despite his demanding career, he always prioritized his role as a loving husband and father. He managed to strike a balance between his professional and personal life, a quality that his colleagues often admired.

Later that day, Dr. Kilani was at St. Peter's hospital, standing in the corner of the trauma reception area while on the phone. He was awaiting an update about his wife's health from Dr. Robert. He wore a sky-blue T-shirt paired with grey chinos and sneakers, a casual but professional look. His deep, smooth voice carried through the quiet corner as he spoke on the phone, a tone that complemented his commanding yet approachable demeanor.

Dr. Kilani was tall and broad-chested, with a presence that naturally drew attention. His intelligence and charm were qualities that Mrs. Kilani often said had first captivated her. Even now, despite the stress of the past few days, his confidence and composure were evident.

As he wrapped up the phone call, the medical receptionist called out his name. He quickly ended his conversation, walking briskly to her desk with an air of expectation.

"Dr. Kilani, Dr. Robert is expecting you in room 112. It's the room to the left at the end of this hallway. Your wife is awake, and she would like to see you," she informed him with a smile.

"Oh … great … thank you," he replied, his tone filled with relief and anticipation. Without hesitation, he headed toward room 112, eager to see his wife.

"My pleasure," she said warmly, watching him stride purposefully down the hallway.

Inside room 112, the atmosphere was calm and sterile, the soft hum of the health monitoring device breaking the silence. The room was modestly furnished with a bed at the center, two chairs neatly positioned for visitors, and a bedside table that held a patient chart and a lampstand with a telephone. A bathroom door stood to the side. The walls were painted a serene sky blue, with a whiteboard mounted on one side. An IV stand with saline bags was placed on the right side of the bed, while the patient health monitoring device stood on the left. Across from the bed was a small closet for storing personal items, and a garbage disposal can sat discreetly nearby.

Mrs. Kilani lay awake, her movements slow but deliberate. A bandage wrapped around her head and right hand hinted at the injuries she had endured in the accident. Scars and abrasions marred parts of her face, neck, and arms, but her eyes carried a quiet resilience.

"Hello, honey!" Dr. Kilani greeted his wife warmly as he moved closer, leaning down to kiss her gently.

"Hello, sweetheart," she replied softly, her voice steady but faint.

"Wow, I'm so glad to see you talking now," he said, his tone filled with relief and excitement.

"Good day, Dr. Robert," he greeted his wife's attending physician, who stood at the foot of the bed.

"Good day, Dr. Kilani," Dr. Robert responded with a professional but kind demeanor.

"Your wife is a very fortunate woman," Dr. Robert began, his expression reassuring. "She sustained multiple cuts on her head and right hand, but the good news is that her head injury report shows only minor contusions—no skull fractures or internal bleeding. There's no evidence of concussion or other significant trauma. Her right arm wounds are also not severe, and there are no broken bones."

"That's incredible news," Dr. Kilani said, his voice reflecting his relief.

"Her response to treatment has been remarkable," Dr. Robert continued a note of optimism in his voice. "If things proceed as expected, she should be discharged earlier than we initially anticipated—let's say sometime next week."

"Wow, that's fantastic. Thank you so much, doctor," Dr. Kilani said, his gratitude evident.

"We'll continue to monitor her health closely and dress her wounds. While her progress is excellent, we need to ensure no underlying issues emerge as a result of the accident.

For that reason, we're keeping her here a little longer for observation," Dr. Robert explained.

"Understood. Thank you again," Dr. Kilani replied, nodding.

"Do you have any questions?" Dr. Robert asked, shifting his gaze between Dr. Kilani and his wife.

Dr. Kilani hesitated briefly before asking, "Since her condition is improving, I'd like to know if she's strong enough to receive visitors. Specifically, just our children."

"Absolutely," Dr. Robert assured him, "but we'll need to keep visits brief and limited to ensure she gets the rest she needs to heal properly from the trauma."

"That's perfectly understandable. Thank you," Dr. Kilani said with a polite smile.

Turning to his patient, Dr. Robert asked, "Mrs. Kilani, do you have any questions or concerns before I leave?"

"No concerns or questions for now. Thank you for everything, Dr. Robert," she replied, her voice conveying quiet gratitude.

"See you later, Mrs. Kilani. Get well soon, and don't hesitate to let us know how you're feeling as the treatment continues," Dr. Robert encouraged before turning to leave.

"Okay … thank you again, bye," Mrs. Kilani replied softly.

"Bye," Dr. Robert responded as he walked out of the room, leaving her to rest.

As the door clicked shut, Andy sat down by his wife's bedside, his concern evident. "How are you feeling, my honey?" he asked, gently holding her left hand.

"You really scared me and the children … I missed you so much," he added, pressing a soft kiss to the back of her hand.

"I missed you too," Mrs. Kilani replied, her voice hoarse but full of warmth.

"How are Milo and Misti? I hope they're not too overwhelmed by all of this," she asked, her worry for them still lingering despite her own pain.

"They're doing well. I told them not to worry too much and that you'd be okay," Andy reassured her, pulling out his phone to send a quick message.

"I'll text them now to come visit after school," he said as he typed a message to Misti and Milo.

"Thank you, sweetheart," Mrs. Kilani murmured, wincing slightly from the pain.

"Sorry, dear," Andy said quickly, brushing her hand gently.

It was half past two, and school had just ended. Students were spilling out in groups, chattering with their friends and heading home. Milo and Misti both grinned when they received the text message from their dad. Milo immediately texted Misti to meet him in the cafeteria so they could head to the hospital together.

At the hospital, the medical receptionist greeted them and directed them to room 112. As they entered, their faces lit up when they saw their mom. They approached her bed gently, their excitement clear.

"Hey … mama!" they both exclaimed in unison, rushing to her side to give her a hug.

"Hi, dad," Milo greeted as he hugged his father.

"Hello, Dad," Misti added, her smile matching her brother's.

"Hello … I hope you both had a good day at school," Andy asked, his voice warm.

"Yes, we did … right, Milo?" Misti said, turning to her brother.

"Yep," Milo confirmed with a grin.

"Hello, my wonders … I've really missed you," Mrs. Kilani said softly, her eyes welling up with emotion as she gazed at her children.

"We really missed you too, Mom," Milo said, kissing her cheek.

"Yeah … mama," Misti echoed, laughing and planting a kiss on her as well.

"How are you feeling now?" Misti asked, brushing her mom's hair gently.

"I'm feeling better," Mrs. Kilani answered, smiling faintly.

"The doctor said that your mother will be out of here soon," Andy added, his voice full of optimism.

"Oh … that's great news!" Milo and Misti both said, their faces lighting up with relief.

"We can't wait for you to come back home, mom," Milo continued. "I've missed your real homemade food," he teased, making Misti giggle.

"What! … what are you trying to say?" Misti asked, her voice playful as she smiled at her brother.

"Thanks to Mrs. Smith, who brings us dinner every night," Milo told their mom with a wink.

"That's very kind of her," Mrs. Kilani said softly, her eyes shining with gratitude.

"Mom … how did the accident happen?" Milo suddenly asked, his curiosity piqued.

"Milo, your mom needs to rest," Andy interjected quickly. "We don't want her to talk about that right now. Don't worry; the right time will come for her to tell us how it happened."

"All right, Dad," Milo replied, nodding in understanding.

After spending some more time with Mrs. Kilani, chatting and making lighthearted jokes, the visiting hours were up. Andy, Milo, and Misti all said their goodbyes and headed back home, their hearts lighter, knowing that their mom was improving.

Chapter Eleven

The prom party had started, and the weather was perfect for the night. It wasn't too cold, nor too hot, but just right for the girls who had chosen to wear short dresses. Most of the girls, however, opted for long dresses in various colors and designs. Their hair, nails, and makeup were all meticulously done, and they looked absolutely stunning. The boys, on the other hand, were dressed in tuxedos or shirts with dress pants. Their hair was neatly groomed, completing their elegant looks.

In the school's auditorium, celebrants of Swiftly High School's prom were chatting excitedly as they made their way inside. Some students stood around near their locker rooms, perfecting their outfits or helping their friends with their last-minute touches. Some boys and girls darted in and out of the restroom, making use of the mirrors to tweak their appearance.

As Misti and her best friend, Elise, entered the restroom to finalize their makeup, they were met by Lindsey and Claire, two girls who were always ready with a snide comment.

"Look who's here," Lindsey said to Claire, her voice dripping with sarcasm. Claire turned her head to see who her friend was referring to.

"It's 'Eclipse' … and the geek!" Lindsey burst into laughter, twisting Elise's name and calling Misti a geek despite the fact that Misti wasn't even wearing her glasses that night.

"Who did both of your makeups? A farmer?" Claire chimed in, followed by more laughter. "You both look ugly," she added.

"Your dresses are ugly, too," Lindsey sneered.

"Nah … nah … something isn't adding up here," Claire continued, shaking her head as if she was making a profound observation.

"Please, tell me what isn't adding up," Misti retorted, her voice calm but sharp. "You're wearing a dress, and we're wearing dresses that are clearly more beautiful than yours. Maybe that's what doesn't add up for you, haters," she snapped back, her words filled with confidence.

"We're all here tonight to have a good time, so why don't you swallow your hate?" Misti continued, standing tall.

"Let's just go to another restroom," Elise whispered, tugging on Misti's hand.

"No," Misti replied firmly, pulling her hand free. "I'm not backing down. Let me confront these haters."

She turned back toward Lindsey and Claire, her tone full of authority. "You both need to get some help with all the negativity you carry around because you're always so miserable. Maybe it's time to look at your own lives and get the mental help you so clearly need."

"Oh … oh!" Some of the other girls in the restroom gasped and laughed at Lindsey and Claire, enjoying the tension.

Misti's words stung, but Lindsey wasn't ready to let it go. "Now you've got the mouth to talk, huh?" she taunted, stepping closer to Misti as though ready to pick a fight.

"We will no longer be intimidated by you," Misti said firmly, standing her ground. "For all our high school years, you've chosen to tease, taunt, and make jokes at our expense. This is our final year, with just a few months left to graduate.

Enough of your madness, don't you think?" she asked, her voice steady but filled with resolve.

Lindsey's eyes narrowed in anger. "I'm going to beat you up," she threatened, stepping closer.

"You can do nothing," Misti replied, her tone cold and unwavering.

"Let's go, Misti," Elise said quietly, tugging at her hand again, sensing the tension building.

Misti shook her head. "Any time you come at me or Elise again, there will be a problem. So stay away from us and let us be," she warned them, standing tall.

As Misti spoke, other girls quickly stepped in between them, attempting to separate the two sides. Elise, seeing the situation escalate, pulled Misti away, guiding her out of the restroom toward another nearby one.

Misti tried to maintain her composure as they walked away. She knew that giving in to anger would only give her haters more power over her. She decided not to let the negativity ruin her night and focused on enjoying the evening with her dear friend, Elise.

Misti wore a stunning floor-length red princess gown designed with lace material around the chest area. Elise looked equally beautiful in a long yellow gown decorated with beads around the waist. The atmosphere in the auditorium was alive with energy—junior and senior students were dancing, chatting, eating, and drinking. Some groups gathered to take photos, while others were snapping selfies. Various games added to the fun, and the sound of laughter filled the air. The DJ kept the excitement alive, playing a mix of upbeat songs that got everyone on the dance floor.

Couples exchanged corsages and boutonnieres, showing affection and love for one another. As the night wore on, the party continued to be a memorable experience for both the juniors and seniors of Swiftly High School, filled with moments of joy and celebration.

The following day, a Sunday, the Kilanis went to visit Mrs. Klara Kilani at the hospital after leaving the church. The trauma waiting room was quieter than it had been in previous days. The weekend medical receptionist attended to a few visitors sitting patiently, waiting to see their loved ones. When the Kilanis approached, they informed her of their visit to Mrs. Kilani. The receptionist let them know that Mrs. Kilani had been moved to the rehabilitation ward for the next phase of her recovery treatment. She directed them to room 205.

"You can take the elevator on your right to the second floor," she instructed kindly.

"All right, thank you," Mr. Kilani replied with a smile, leading Misti and Milo toward the elevator.

Mrs. Kilani was sitting on the bed, watching TV, when her family arrived. They were all relieved and happy to see her recovering so well. She was making significant progress. Klara smiled at them and shared the good news that the doctor had set her discharge date for Wednesday of that week. This was the moment they had all been eagerly waiting for.

"I am thankful to God that I'm alive," Klara told her family, her voice full of gratitude.

"We are thankful as well," they replied, equally relieved.

"Everything happened so fast that I didn't have the chance to think things through," Klara continued thoughtfully.

"On my way home that day, I didn't check the weather to see that it was going to rain. Otherwise, I would've just stayed home," she reflected, looking down.

"You know, the Center Farms Place is about ten miles away, and I went there to get some freshly harvested produce. You know how it works over there—you go to the farm, pick what you want, and then pay for it," she explained.

"Oh, that place," her husband said, nodding. "The roads are muddy even on a dry day. I can only imagine how bad they must've been when it rained. You could have gotten the produce from somewhere closer instead of driving so far," he pointed out.

"I know, but the fresh produce tastes so much better when it's just been harvested," Klara insisted.

"True, but look where that decision led us," her husband replied gently.

"Please, Mom, continue," Misti urged, her impatience growing as she wanted to know more.

"So, I was on the farm, plucking the produce I needed," Klara resumed. "As I was doing that, it started to drizzle. I checked my weather app, and it warned of a thunderstorm in the area and surrounding regions," she recounted.

"When I saw that, I quickly wrapped up, paid for my produce, and started heading home," she continued. "But then, the rain started pouring down so heavily that I couldn't see. The trees along the road only made things worse, blocking my visibility."

Mrs. Kilani's voice quivered as she recalled the incident. "I tried my best to drive carefully and get to the main tarred road, but I didn't see the deer crossing the road until it was too late. I swerved to avoid hitting it, and the car skidded, going straight into a small ditch on the side of the muddy road. That was the last thing I remember before everything went black," she said, tears welling in her eyes.

"Oh, Mom, that must have been so hard," Milo said softly, his voice full of sorrow, as he wrapped his arm around her.

"Yes, it was," she responded, her voice shaky as she sniffled, trying to control her emotions.

"It's okay, Mom," Misti said soothingly, reaching over to hug her. "You're still here with us, and that's what matters."

Her husband patted her shoulder gently. "It's all right, darling," he reassured her, offering comfort in his embrace.

"The first day I opened my eyes and saw myself in the hospital, I was completely confused by all the bandages on my head and arm," Mrs. Kilani continued, her voice trembling slightly. "The attending nurse was in the room at the time. She explained that I had been brought in after an accident."

She paused, looking at her family with a soft, distant gaze. "The first thing I thought about was all of you. I honestly thought I wouldn't see you again," she said, her voice breaking as tears filled her eyes.

"I thought I wasn't going to see you again," she repeated quietly, wiping a tear from her cheek.

"It's okay… We're here, and you're here with us, too," her husband reassured her, his voice filled with tenderness. "We thank God for that."

Klara took a deep breath, her mind still processing everything. "Who found me in the ditch?" she asked, her voice still shaky.

"We heard from the police that it was a good Samaritan—someone who was also coming home from the farm. They saw your car in the ditch and called 9-1-1," her husband explained.

Klara nodded, relieved that someone had helped. "So, what happened to my car?" she asked.

"It's been towed to the mechanic's shop," her husband reassured her. "Don't worry about that. It's taken care of. The only thing we want is for you to rest and focus on your recovery."

"Oh, okay… Thank you," she said, her voice softer now as she gave him a weak smile.

Klara's emotional account of the accident and her recovery left her family deeply moved. They surrounded her with love and comfort, grateful to have her back with them. She was thankful to be alive, to be a wife and a mother, and to have been given a second chance to be with her family.

The days passed quickly, and three days later, she was discharged from the hospital. At home, friends and sympathizers from work, church, and their community came to visit, sharing in the joy of her recovery. The Kilanis were filled with hope, looking forward to the silver lining that would come from such a challenging experience.

Chapter Twelve

A new club was formed by the student affairs committee of Swiftly High School to address growing concerns about the social and emotional well-being of students. Every Wednesday after school, students from both Swiftly High School and Swiftly Middle School gathered in the school auditorium for a unique social laboratory club called "Speak Out." This club was established to provide a safe, supportive, and inclusive environment where students could openly share and address the personal challenges they faced at home, school, religious gatherings, online, and in other areas of their lives. It was the first initiative of its kind in the district, reflecting the school administration's commitment to fostering emotional resilience and community among students.

The club's purpose went beyond simple conversation. One of its main focuses was to uncover the root causes of students' problems—be it bullying, academic pressure, peer influence, or family dynamics—and then work collaboratively on solutions. The approach emphasized building empathy, understanding, and actionable steps, ensuring students felt heard and empowered to tackle their challenges. To complement this, the club's operations were designed with confidentiality and communication in mind. At the end of each meeting, the Swiftly School student affairs committee sent out a carefully crafted email to parents, summarizing the broad topics and issues discussed while strictly avoiding naming or identifying any specific students. This transparency allowed parents to stay informed about the pressures their children might be facing and encouraged them to initiate meaningful conversations at home.

On the school's side, issues that fell within its purview, such as incidents of bullying or challenges with specific policies, were investigated and addressed promptly by the administration. The collaborative model created a feedback loop between students, parents, and the school, making "Speak Out" a cornerstone of student well-being.

Ms. Jones, a compassionate and well-respected teacher with a background in social work and student counseling, served as the club advisor. She oversaw the club's activities, ensuring a nurturing and respectful atmosphere. Under her guidance, students were encouraged to speak freely, knowing they were in a judgment-free zone. The club's slogan, "What happens here, stays here," underscored the importance of trust and loyalty within the group. This mantra became a cornerstone of the club, helping to build a sense of belonging and security among its members.

To foster a welcoming environment, each meeting began with an introduction for new attendees. Ms. Jones made it a point to engage with every student, recognizing that stepping into such a space for the first time could feel intimidating. The meetings were structured yet flexible, allowing students to share their thoughts, experiences, and concerns openly, with their peers offering support and validation. The overall goal was to empower students to navigate life's challenges more effectively and to build a resilient, empathetic school community.

"Attention, everyone. Good day, and welcome to this week's meeting. This is S-p-e-a-k... Out," Ms. Jones announced enthusiastically, her voice filling the school auditorium as the buzz of chatter among the students died down. Her tone was warm and inviting, immediately setting a safe and inclusive atmosphere.

"Good day, Ms. Jones," the students responded in unison, their voices echoing back.

"Do we have any first-time attendees here today?" she asked, scanning the room with a smile that encouraged participation. Her approachable demeanor always made it easier for students to feel comfortable, even if they were nervous about opening up.

"If this is your first time attending this club, we want to formally recognize and welcome you," she added. Her words were followed by a short pause as a group of new students, both from middle and high school, hesitantly stood up. The rest of the club members erupted into applause, creating a wave of warmth and encouragement. Some of the regular attendees even cheered lightly, making the newcomers grin shyly but appreciatively.

"Without wasting much time, do we have anyone who would like to share today?" Ms. Jones asked, her hands gesturing toward the crowd as she opened the floor. To her surprise, several hands shot up, eager to share. She glanced around the room, her expression one of quiet pride at the willingness of the students to speak up. She pointed to the first raised hand.

A middle school student stood up, her small frame trembling slightly as she adjusted her posture. "I was bullied today in class by a classmate," she began hesitantly, her voice trembling but clear. "She called me a 'fat pig.' That really hurt." The room grew quiet as her words hung in the air. "I reported it to my teacher, but she denied it. The teacher couldn't do anything because I couldn't prove it," she added, her gaze dropping to the floor as she finished.

Ms. Jones' face softened, and she nodded empathetically. "Thank you for sharing that with us," she said, her voice steady but filled with kindness. "I want you to know that what happened to you is not okay. Nobody deserves to be treated that way. I will make sure the school investigates this situation thoroughly," she assured the student, her tone resolute.

Pausing briefly, Ms. Jones leaned forward slightly as if to emphasize her next words. "And let me tell you something: you are beautiful just the way you are. Your worth is not determined by someone else's hurtful words."

The room erupted into applause as the other students clapped and cheered in solidarity. Some shouted words of encouragement like "You're amazing!" and "Ignore the haters!" The middle school student looked up, her cheeks slightly red from the attention, but there was a small, genuine smile on her face.

Another student was called to share their experience. A tall, shy-looking high schooler with dark hair and a hesitant gaze stood up, nervously clutching the edge of their desk.

"Someone sent me a hate message yesterday through my social media direct messages," he began, his voice trembling slightly. The room grew silent as he continued, the weight of his words sinking in. "He called me a 'terrorist' because of my profile picture. That remark ruined my day yesterday," he explained, his voice heavy with emotion.

Ms. Jones' face softened with compassion. "First of all, thank you for sharing this with us. I know it's not easy to talk about such things," she said, her tone gentle yet firm. "You know you are a handsome young man with a gentle soul. Did you block the person from messaging you again?" she asked him, her eyes meeting his in a reassuring way.

"Yes, I did immediately," the student replied, nodding. "But the remark stayed in my head. I can't stop thinking about it." His voice quivered slightly, betraying the depth of the hurt he felt.

Ms. Jones offered a warm, understanding smile. "All right," she said, turning her attention to the rest of the group. "Let's help him get that negative remark out of his head with some positive words. Are we ready?"

The students didn't hesitate. They stood up, their voices rising in unison. "You're amazing!" one shouted. "You're strong!" another chimed in. "You're kind, and that's what matters!" a third called out. The room filled with uplifting chants and affirmations as the student slowly began to smile, the support of his peers clearly lifting his spirits.

Ms. Jones let the moment linger before she called on another student to share. A high school student with a somber expression stood up. His shoulders slumped slightly, and he avoided eye contact as he began to speak.

"In my case," he said, his voice tinged with sadness, "my parents compare me to my older brother in terms of academic performance. They make me feel like I'm worthless. I'm trying my best… I guess it's just not enough." His words hung heavily in the air, and a few students nodded in quiet understanding.

Ms. Jones walked closer to the student, her voice calm and empathetic. "Thank you for being brave enough to share this with us. I want you to know that this comparison issue has been brought up by other students as well. It's something we're paying close attention to," she assured him.

Pausing briefly, she continued, "A communication will be sent to all parents regarding this very point. I want you to know that you are not alone in feeling this way. You are unique and valuable, just as you are. Keep doing your best, but please don't pressure yourself into thinking you have to be someone else. Be proud of who you are because there is only one you, and that's your strength."

The room broke into applause as the other students clapped enthusiastically. Several chimed in with kind words, saying, "You're doing great!" and "Don't let anyone make you feel less than amazing!"

The student's somber expression softened as he nodded in appreciation, visibly comforted by the outpouring of support from his peers.

Another student was called up to share their story. A middle school boy with a nervous fidget approached the front of the group. His hands trembled slightly as he gripped the microphone, his eyes darting around the room before focusing on Ms. Jones.

"Hello, everyone," he began, his voice barely audible at first. He took a deep breath, encouraged by the attentive silence of the room. "I met a group of guys through a friend who lives in my area. At first, it seemed harmless—we'd play basketball together after school. But then things started to change. They introduced me to doing drugs and other bad things. I refused to join them, but now they're threatening to beat me up if I cross their path because I said no. I feel anxious about leaving my house. Even coming to school has become a big deal for me," he explained, his voice quivering as he poured out his feelings.

Ms. Jones nodded empathetically, her expression a mix of concern and support. "Thank you for sharing this with us," she began, her voice steady and reassuring. "This is a very serious issue, and I want you to know that you are incredibly brave for standing your ground and refusing to get involved in those activities. Have you told your parents about what's been going on?"

The boy hesitated, his gaze dropping to the floor. "My parents don't have time to listen," he said, his voice tinged with frustration and sadness. "Even when they do, they just blame me for getting involved with the group in the first place instead of helping me. I joined them to play basketball. At first, it was fun. But after a while, they started talking about getting narcotics and stuff. When I said no, I stopped hanging out with them… and now they're angry at me," he explained, his voice trailing off.

Ms. Jones walked closer to the student, her tone gentle yet firm. "I'm sorry you're going through this, but I want you to know you did the right thing by refusing to get involved with drugs and distancing yourself from them," she said. "This situation is not your fault. You shouldn't have to face this alone, and you deserve support from your parents and your community."

She turned to address the room. "Everyone, let's show him some love for being strong and making the right choices," she said. The room erupted into applause, with students shouting, "You're so brave!" and "We're proud of you!" Some students even stood up to clap louder, the energy in the room buzzing with encouragement.

Ms. Jones returned her attention to the boy. "The school will share this information with the other parents to help raise awareness of what's happening in our community. Additionally, we'll reach out to your parents to help them understand the seriousness of this situation and the need to support you," she promised.

The boy nodded, his expression a mixture of relief and gratitude. For the first time during his speech, he managed a small, tentative smile.

As the meeting continued, more students shared their personal challenges and pressures. Each story brought a wave of empathy and support from the group, reinforcing the club's sense of community and solidarity.

Misti and Milo sat quietly among the students, listening intently to each story. While they didn't share anything during this session, their presence added to the collective spirit of support that defined the Speak Out club.

As the meeting drew to a close, Ms. Jones stood at the front of the room, her warm smile radiating pride and appreciation for the students' bravery and honesty. Together, she and the students chanted, "What happens here, stays here," their voices echoing with unity and trust as the meeting ended.